PRESENCE

Community

***Being the Church** instead of
Going to Church*

PRESENCE-BASED
Community

Being the Church instead of
Going to Church

JON QUESENBERRY

Paperback ISBN 978-1-7367912-0-2
eBook ISBN 978-1-73679125-1-9

Publishing and Printing Services provided by
Orison Publishers, Inc.
PO Box 188, Grantham, PA 17027
www.OrisonPublishers.com

DEDICATION

I want to dedicate this book to my wife Carol, who persevered with me through many trials and who continually reveals the love and character of God to me. She is my partner and closest friend.

I also want to dedicate this book to my parents Joseph and Lois Quesenberry, who loved me by teaching me the Word of God, equipping me to worship and providing me with an example by daily seeking the face of God in prayer.

I also want to acknowledge Thom Gardner, a good friend and counselor. Without Thom, I would have never written this book. He loved me and pointed me in the right direction. He gave me hope and guided me toward the goal of yieldedness when I didn't even know what it was.

FOREWORD

There was a time in my life when everything changed. I had been a pastor and church planter for fourteen years. My wife and I had successfully planted a church in 2001. More than a hundred people called the church home. We had great meetings and enjoyed wonderful fellowship. We were a successful community church that supported missionaries, put on annual conferences and hosted outreach and discipleship programs. Even though everything seemed to be going well, I found myself empty and distracted. During what seemed to be a prosperous time in ministry, I felt that I had lost my way and that I was very far away from God.

In November of 2011, I announced to my church that I would be stepping down from being their pastor. I told them that I was in need of a time of healing. I informed them that I would continue to attend, but that I would not be involved in leadership. In February of 2012, I formally resigned. During the following two years, I experienced a dramatic shift in my orientation and attitude toward everything in my life, particularly my relationship with God.

Prior to that time, I would say that I *served* God and *loved* people. I realized that my relationship with God was secondary to my relationship with others. God began teaching me how to *love* Him first and and *serve* people.

I *did* hear the voice of God in my ministry, but I realized that I was not yielded. Instead of living like Jesus, who said, "I only do what I see the Father doing" (John 5:19), I sought God for the fulfillment of my own needs. I didn't seek God to enjoy His expressions of love and encouragement for me. Many times I would sense the Lord leading me into situations and speaking to me in ways that challenged my desires. Over and over again, I simply hesitated. I didn't rebel; I just simply refused to deny myself. Instead, I often did what I thought was best. At times I grieved the Spirit of God by purposefully sinning.

It was through these experiences of grieving and quenching the Spirit of God in my life that I lost my way. During this time, when I sinned, I asked God to forgive me, but there was no relief. I found myself powerless in certain situations. I was caught in a pattern of sinning and repenting over and over again. It seemed as though I was powerless to change. I had lost track of the path of living for God that I was walking on and just could not easily find it. I became aware that I needed an entirely new relationship with God. It seemed clear that I could not just turn the page and start again as I had done several times before. It was obvious to me that I could not continue in the way that I was going. I needed to find my way back to where I had started with God. I needed to rekindle my first love.

I was working three, twelve-hour shifts as a registered nurse at the local hospital, so I had four days each week that I was not working. On these days, I began to study my Bible and pray for several hours each day. At first I just cried out to God with tears to forgive me for past sins. I believed it would just be a matter of time until healing would come and I would be restored to ministry. The only thing positive I felt in response to my confession was a full assurance of forgiveness. This reassurance was amazing, but I still felt lost.

After many days of confession and repentance, I began to pour out the frustrations that I felt to the Lord. I cried out with all that I had to the Lord, telling Him the needs that I had. After many days, I noticed that nothing changed. So I began to claim the promises of God instead. This change lasted just a short while because it made me feel even worse.

I was in a very difficult place. I could sense the presence of God in the room, but it was as if He just was not talking to me. I knew that He was not angry. I knew that He was not absent, but I felt no real connection with Him. Then I began to cry out in frustration. For days I laid my heart bare to God, expressing the deepest desires of my heart to Him. I told Him that I no longer wanted to be a pastor. I told Him that I was finished doing what I wanted and that I would do whatever He told me to do! I was hoping that this confession would repair the brokenness between us. Nothing changed.

For days, emotionally and spiritually broken, I poured out my heart. My times in prayer increased. The transparency I had with the Lord felt good, but I still heard no reply. Instead, the silence continued with no breakthrough. After several weeks of crying out to God in this way, I began to spend hours lying on the floor. At times I would simply say, "I'm Yours…." Because I felt His presence in the room, just being quiet in that place became encouraging enough.

My times of waiting on the Lord increased. Occasionally I would say, "I'm here…." When troubling thoughts came, I called out, "Help me…." My prayer life was reduced to short two-word prayers and long periods of watching and waiting. During this time, many Scriptures came to mind. I began reading sections of the Bible where God had a personal relationship with certain people, particularly Adam, Abraham, Moses and, of course, Jesus. My orientation to God began to change. The way that I interpreted Scriptures began to change. The passionate and intimate writings of David in the Psalms and of the disciple "whom Jesus loved" in the Book of John began to come alive. The Bible changed from being the Word of God that needed to be studied into the very words of God whispered in my ear. He began to tell me about His great love for me and His thoughts for me.

Almost a year had passed and I was sitting at my desk studying the words of Jesus on the cross when my heart just simply broke through in surrender. I spontaneously said out loud, "From now on, Lord, I will listen to Your voice. If You are telling me to do it, I will. If You tell me not to do it, then I won't. If You are silent, then I will wait."

Out of this experience and in response to my promise to the Lord, this book was written.

CONTENTS

Section One

PRINCIPLES OF PRESENCE-BASED COMMUNITY

Chapter One
THE
PERSONHOOD
OF GOD

W e know that God created the whole world using His Word alone. Although God's Word was sufficient to form the cosmos, the creation of humanity was entirely a personal and intimate event. The Bible tells us that, "God formed a man from the dust of the ground and breathed into his nostrils the breath of life, and the man became a living being" (Genesis 2:7 NIV).

Adam was created and enlivened by the presence of God. The hands of God surrounded Adam as he was formed from the dust of the earth. The mouth of God was upon Adam when he received his life-giving spirit. Adam's inception to the world was in a face-to-face encounter with the presence of God. This is the origin of presence-based community.

In His Image
Just before the creation of Adam, God made a declaration. He said, "Let us make mankind in our *image*, [and] in our *likeness*..." (Genesis 1:26 NIV, emphasis added). In this way God announced the plan for His creation. Without a knowledge of the original language, we might think that the use of the words *image* and *likeness* in this passage are poetic.

Instead, the meanings of these two words are quite different, and their individual meanings provide profound insight into the intentions of God for humanity. God's creation of humanity is not only about the design of Adam, but also about the revelation of God Himself!

The Hebrew word translated as "image" is fairly straightforward. It literally means "*resemblance*; a representative *figure*."[1] The word translated *image* simply means to make one thing in the shape of the other. If we are to interpret this word literally. then it means Adam was created in the shape of God with arms, legs, face and hands, etc., because God Himself has these features!

What does it mean to us that God has a face, hands and feet like we do? If we truly believe that God made us "like" Himself (in His image and likeness), then He has eyes like us and we can understand that He can see us. If, like us, God has ears, then He can hear us. In fact, His careful attention at creation indicates that He wants to know us and to be intimate with us. If, like us, God has a face and hands—hands that He used to form and enliven the first human—then perhaps we were created to see His face and experience His touch.

The Hebrew word for "likeness" is a little bit more complicated. There is some discussion around the true meaning of this word, but one of the most common (and literal) ways to interpret the Hebrew word for "likeness" is "like fashion, manner, similitude."[2] This unique word is only used twenty-two times in the Bible and seems to describe more about the character of an object rather than it's shape.

What does it mean to humanity if we are indeed made in the character of God Himself? What does it mean that God formed us according to His "character"? Does this mean that God created us with a mind, a will and emotions like Himself? If we believe—as the Scriptures report—that human beings were made with great care and attention according to the pattern of God, then we must believe that God has a mind, will and emotions that function similar to that of humanity. If this is true, then God has thoughts in His mind about us. God has a plan in His will for us and, of course, God has love in His heart (emotions) for us.

The most confirming thing about this interpretation is that the descriptions of God in the Bible confirm this understanding! According to the Bible, God is described as having human features. He has a face because we are commanded to "seek His face" (Psalm 105:4 NKJV). God has hands because He uses them to deliver Israel from the Egyptians (Exodus 7:5). Our God has eyes because Noah "found favor in the eyes of the LORD" (Genesis 6:8 NIV). God has a voice because several have reported hearing Him speak. (Ezekiel 43:2 in the New International Version tell us that His voice sounds "like the roar of rushing waters"!) According to other Scriptures recorded by people having divine encounters, God also has ears, arms, feet, fingers, head, hair, heart, legs, a neck and shoulders. Moses even reported seeing God's back (Exodus 33:23)!

In His likeness
The Bible reports that God *thinks about us, has plans for us, and knows us* even before we are born. He is moved with compassion. He also gets angry. He is full of love and joy, and at times He can experience jealousy! (See Jeremiah 1:5; 12:15; 29:11; Numbers 32:10; 1 John 4:8; Isaiah 62:5 and Joshua 24:19.)

The *Oxford Dictionary* defines *personality* as "the combination of characteristics or qualities that form an individual's distinctive character."[3] Using this definition, we can say that God certainly does have a personality. But this is not a new theology that distracts from the divinity of God; instead, it is a biblical affirmation of the way that God desires to be known!

In fact, the Bible reveals that our God is One in three Persons! This statement, although it is a complete mystery, continues to be the centerpiece of Christian theology. The Apostles' Creed, written in 325 C.E., expressly affirms the personhood of God in this way:

> I believe in God, the Father Almighty, Creator of Heaven and earth; and in Jesus Christ, His only Son our Lord, who was conceived by the Holy Spirit...I believe in the Holy Spirit....

Jesus consistently chose to communicate with God in very personal terms, calling Him "My Father" and "Abba," meaning "Daddy." This familiarity with God was so offensive to the religious leaders of His day that they listed it as legal grounds for His crucifixion.

...they tried all the more to kill him; not only was he breaking the Sabbath, but he was even calling God his own Father, making himself equal with God. (John 5:18 NIV)

It cannot be underestimated how offensive it was to the religious people to hear Jesus speak to God in such an intimate way. Their understanding of God was based on a very different understanding of His character. Instead of encouraging the view of God as accessible, the Pharisees taught that God was holy and unapproachable and that obedience to His laws was the way to sustain His blessing and favor.

As it turns out, the Bible is full of descriptions about the nature of God's personality. The Scriptures record that the patriarchs interacted with God face to face; the Old Testament is full of descriptions about God and His personality.

The Bible says that "the LORD would speak to Moses face to face, as one speaks to a friend..." (Exodus 33:11 NIV). Moses's interaction on Mount Sinai reveals many details. During one of these face-to-face encounters, the Lord describes to Moses His character qualities in great detail:

And he passed in front of Moses, proclaiming, "The LORD, the LORD, the compassionate and gracious God, slow to anger, abounding in love and faithfulness, maintaining love to thousands, and forgiving wickedness, rebellion and sin. Yet he does not leave the guilty unpunished.... (Exodus 34:6-7 NIV)

The personality traits of God are well documented; for example, He is holy, wise and faithful. He is patient, merciful and kind. He is all-knowing, all-powerful and always present to His people. He is outrageously creative and loves to amaze us with what He does. He is both incredibly orderly and chaotic. He is familiar and enigmatic, with a way that continually arouses our interest and affection. Just the descriptive names given to God in the Bible, the ones describing His nature, number in the hundreds! Rather than being an impersonal force, God is a person, and He has made Himself "personal" so we can know Him. He wants to be known.

4

God reveals that although He is *One*, He is *three* Persons: Father, Son and Holy Spirit. Each personage exists in community with full possession of all the characteristics and qualities of God—a divine community existing in seamless communion.

The Habitation of God

Father God lovingly presides over the universe. The Bible in several different passages describes that He is seated in the heavenlies (Isaiah 6:1; 66:1; Psalm 103:19; Daniel 7:9; Matthew 5:34; Revelation 4:1-6). From this place He attentively and creatively sustains the earth and cosmos. The fullness of His creative personality and power is majestically revealed in creation. Although He is always at work, He operates from a place of rest. He is surrounded in glory, wonder and worship, full of careful attention to all that He has created. God is love. (See John 5:17; Romans 1:20; Hebrews 4:4 and Revelation 4:2-11.)

Jesus is a person, fully God and fully man, seated "at the right hand" of the Father in the heavenlies (Ephesians 1:20 NKJV). He is the "only begotten Son" of God (John 1:18 NKJV). He is the Word of God that created the world; through Him all things exist (John 1:3; Romans 11:36). Jesus is the "radiance of God's glory and the exact representation of his being" (Hebrews 1:3 NIV).

Jesus lived on the earth in human form, as a man, to reveal the nature and character of God to humanity. He lived a purposeful and powerful life in lockstep fellowship and obedience to Father God, experiencing all the limitations that we endure yet without sin. He did this as an example to show us what a life lived in communion with and yielded to the presence of God looks like. After laying His life down, God raised Him to life again to be seated in the heavenlies once more. Jesus is seated in the heavens, is worshipped by angels and now serves as the mediator between humanity and the Father. (See Philippians 2:7-8; Luke 9:22; 22:69; John 1:14; 5:19; 10:15; 13:15; Colossians 3:1; Hebrews 4:15 and Revelation 5:11-14.)

The Spirit of God, however, is not seated in the heavenlies. The habitation of the Spirit of God is on the earth! From the first chapter of the Bible to the last, Scripture reveals that when God is present and active on the earth, it is by His Spirit. The Spirit of God was active on the earth starting with the *first* chapter of the *first* book and continues to the *last* chapter of the *last* book in the Bible. In the first chapter of Genesis, Scripture says, "In the beginning God created the heavens and the earth. …the *Spirit of God was hovering* over the face of the waters" (Genesis 1:1-2 NKJV, emphasis added). In the last chapter of Revelation, Scripture says, "The Spirit and the bride say, 'Come!' And let the one who hears say, 'Come!'…" (Revelation 22:17 NIV).

God is present and active on the earth by His Spirit in both the Old and New Testaments. The role of the Spirit of God in the Bible is immanent and personal. God's Spirit is intimately present with His people to *contend* with them (Genesis 6:3); *instruct* them (Nehemiah 9:20); *guide* them (Isaiah 63:11); *give wisdom* (Deuteronomy 34:9); and to *give them peace* (Isaiah 63:14). These are just a few of the Old Testament references! There are many more in the New Testament.

Presence-based community **begins** *with the presence of God.* Since God has made us like Himself and since His desire is to be among us, a presence-based community is in the heart of God. It is now our opportunity to gather around His presence on the earth and participate with Him, to be a community led and empowered by His presence among us.

Chapter Two

PARTNERS
WITH GOD

P artnership is the plan of God. God's plan from the beginning was to enable humanity to participate as partners with Him rather than as puppets to be controlled by Him. To provide Adam with the ability to choose, God gave Adam authority over all creation.

> *Then God blessed them, and God said to them, "Be fruitful and multiply; fill the earth and **subdue it; have dominion over the fish of the sea, over the birds of the air, and over every living thing that moves on the earth.**" (Genesis 1:28 NKJV, emphasis added)*

God did not retain His right to rule but delegated it to humanity. Along with the delegation of this authority to reign, humanity also gained free will. The *Oxford Dictionary* defines free will as "the power of acting without the constraint of necessity; the ability to act at one's own discretion."[1] The ability to exercise dominion on the earth requires free will. How would Adam exercise this delegated authority if he were constrained to the will of God alone? By giving full authority over the "earthly realm" to Adam and Eve, God gave humanity the ability to choose to partner with God or not.

God had created an immense and complex living earth full of amazing creatures, deep oceans and vast resources according to His will. God also had a destiny for the earth. He had and continues to have incredible plans and purposes for the earth—in fact, for all creation. Why would God give humanity full and unbounded authority over the earth when He, Himself, possesses the knowledge needed to accomplish His plans and purposes for it? Why would an omnipotent God full of wisdom and divine power hand over His rule to finite humans with little knowledge and minimal ability to rule the earth? Did God expect Adam to rule the earth without a knowledge of His plans for the earth? Did God think that humanity would be able to steward the earth using their finite abilities and limited knowledge alone? Of course not! God gave Adam full authority on the earth because it was His design and His pleasure to *partner* with him! It was God's plan to do the "heavy lifting" so that Adam and Eve and their children would enjoy the fruits of His perfect plan. The Bible tells us that it is His great love for us that causes Him to desire this partnership (Ephesians 2:3-6).

God wants to partner with humanity to reveal His glory and to extend His Kingdom on the earth. He wants us not only to experience the joy of the success of natural work but also to experience the success of participating with Him in His supernatural work! Although humans are given the capacity to act as lone agents; to discover, by trial and error, which efforts lead to life and which lead to death, this is not the plan of God for humanity. God's deepest desire is that we partner with Him in yielded communion so we can discover His abundant life and enjoy the amazing things that He has created us for! In fact, "Eye has not seen, and ear has not heard, nor has it risen up in the heart of man, the things that God has prepared for those that love Him." (I Corinthians 2:9 LITV)

The First Partnership

When God gave authority to Adam on the earth, God gave Adam the right to rule as if he were "seated...in the heavenly places" (Ephesians 1:20 NKJV), reigning *with* Him on the earth.

The first work of partnership between God and Adam was to name the animals. The Bible tells us that God brought the animals to Adam "to see what he would name them; and whatever the man called each living creature, that was its name" (Genesis 2:19 NIV). For many years, I wondered about the importance of this story in the biblical text. Why would a story about God helping Adam name the animals be important enough to be put in the Bible? I believe that this story is to illustrate the *nature* of the partnership God designed for humanity from the beginning.

God brought the animals to Adam. This was something Adam was unable to do. Then Adam gave the animal a name. This is, of course, something that Adam could do without God's help. Then God *agreed* with the name that Adam had given them. God's agreement was affirmation of the work being done by Adam. God always works with humanity on the earth by agreement. This is how God shows respect for our authority.

Although God owns everything (including Adam), God had chosen to serve Adam by partnering with him. He allowed the man to be successful by assisting him to do what Adam was unable to do. Adam could not have gathered all the animals on the earth one by one and then named them by himself. He only had to participate in *God's plan* to accomplish things that were beyond his ability to do.

A Parable of Partnership

When my son was sixteen years old, he saved some money and together he and I purchased an old, yet reliable, Toyota Camry with a manual transmission. My son and his friends called it "The Rusted Hotness" because even though it was nothing to look at, it ran like a dream! Since we agreed that I would be the one to insure the car, the title was placed in my name. This arrangement assured that I retained ownership of the car. We agreed that even though I technically owned the car, my teenage son would have authority over its use!

In the following months, I took my son out in the parking lot with his "new car" to practice. I remember the first day I sat next to my son in the passenger seat. I remember the relinquishment required to allow him to have full control. I explained how to press down on the clutch and then carefully place the car in gear. I remember that the first few times the car jerked suddenly, stalled and then came to an abrupt stop. After a few tries it seemed to come naturally to my son. I was happy and felt very gratified to see how my coaching was able to allow him to succeed in driving the car.

My son used that car to go everywhere, including several trips out of state! I was amazed at how he took care of it. He kept it neat and clean and full of gas. For all practical purposes, it was *his* car to do with as he liked. In reality it was my car, but I chose not to demand my rights of ownership. I did drive my son's car a few times, but only after asking him if I could drive it! Our partnership was one of full benefit for him, even though he was actually just a steward of the car. He could have driven it over a cliff if he had wanted to! This would have been ludicrous, however, because whatever he did to the car would affect him rather than me.

In accordance with his interest, I taught my son how to maintain the car. I showed him how to check the oil and change the oil and the oil filter. We did it together the first time, then after that he was able to do it himself.

One day, the engine didn't seem to be working properly. After trying to solve the problem himself, he asked if I could help him find the problem and fix it. As it turned out, the "Rusted Hotness" needed a new alternator. Because it was my car, he asked me if I would help him repair it. Because the car was mine, I paid for the repairs. Later on, it needed new tires. He consulted with me again. This time, we decided that I would loan him some of the money that he needed to buy new tires, which I gladly did. My son actually took the car with him when he left for college. During the whole time that he had access to the car, he acknowledged that he benefitted from the partnership that we had. As it turned out, the partnership we had over the car was one that brought us closer. Instead of being something that separated us, working on the car together made us close friends.

Partners in Proximity
Similar to the situation with my son, God has placed us in a situation where we benefit—a situation where we are fully satisfied and enjoy

benefits that are beyond what we can do by ourselves when we are in partnership with Him. He owns the earth while we have been given authority over it. We can do whatever we want, but some of these decisions lead to difficulty and even hardship (or perhaps death). If we live in a yielded relationship with Him, we enjoy His presence with us and what He enables us to do will be the best outcome. In fact, because of His great love, the plans He has for us are always the highest and best. Partnering with God will always stretch us, and we will live in ways that we never dreamed possible.

This is the pattern of partnership. God does not force anyone to do anything. Instead, He stands patiently with plans to bless and partner with us in order to produce amazing results that are completely outside of our will alone. God has chosen not to override the decisions that every person makes. If destructive decisions are made, it grieves His heart, but the consequences are ours to bear. Even then, He is there to lift us up if we turn away (repent) from our own way to follow His ways.

We know that God continues to demonstrate His presence on the earth. He reveals His invisible qualities and His power in creation. His presence remains, but still He limits His divine power over humanity. Paul wrote:

> *For since the creation of the world God's invisible qualities—his eternal power and divine nature—have been clearly seen, being understood from what has been made, so that people are without excuse.* (Romans 1:20 NIV)

This Scripture passage is truly amazing. It declares that God's "invisible qualities" and His "divine nature" *can* be known through partnership in study of the natural world. Sir Isaac Newton was perhaps the most influential scientist of all time. His capacity for understanding and discovery seemed limitless. His accomplishments in mathematics, physics, optics and chemistry were ground-breaking. Newton was a passionate lover of God. His passion for the "counsel and dominion" of God led him into partnership and discovery. In 1824 he wrote, "This most beautiful system of the sun, planets, and comets, could only proceed from the counsel and dominion of an intelligent and powerful Being...."[2]

In Isaiah's vision, the seraphim declare "the whole earth is full of his glory" (Isaiah 6:3 NIV). It is the height of vanity, denial and foolishness to believe that the delicate and complex balance of nature that surrounds us has any other source than intelligent design. Even those who don't believe in God are forced to acknowledge "Mother Nature" as a place card for God in their speech. Truly the earth reveals the presence of God and His desire to be known.

In spite of the revelation of His power on the earth, God chooses relationship over domination. Instead of doing whatever He wants, God has chosen to live and work in close proximity with humanity. He has created a situation that allows humanity to see and experience what He is like in creation, calling people to partner with Him to experience the fullness of His glorious plan on the earth.

Distractions from Partnership

There are two philosophies that resist the idea of partnership with God: *deism* and *fatalism*. Both of these ideologies reject the notion that God has made relationship and partnership with humanity central to His plan.

Deism proposes that God is an impersonal force that set the world in motion. The God of deism cannot be known by personal experience or encounter. This impersonal force cannot exist in partnership with humanity; instead, humans are left on their own to live according to reason and experimentation with the created world. The glory of God is revealed by the circadian rhythms of the earth, the orderly procession of the seasons, and even the instinctive migrations of animals. However, in contrast to deism, God has plans that are to benefit all of humanity in partnership with Him. He desires to partner with humanity in government, business, education, entertainment, arts, communication and the home. All of these spheres are His creation. If at any time a person, nation or people group partners with His divine principles, a certain measure of success results. If humans work in partnership (in yielded relationship) in these areas, the benefit to all is beyond knowing.

The Bible and all accurate historical records reveal that partnership with God changes history.

Fatalism, on the other hand, is the belief that all events are predetermined and therefore inevitable. The Bible also contradicts this ideology. All of us have heard well-meaning believers say, "God is in control!" Although this is true when God is "given control" by humans, this is actually an incorrect way to understand the world around us. According to the Bible, God is not in control of the earth! Humans are! If God were in control, then there would be no war, no hunger and little hardship. If God were truly in control of the earth, then all people everywhere would live in the blessings of Eden. People who say that "God is in control" are actually expressing a fatalistic view of the world which is not biblical. If we are to be biblical believers, we must understand that the control of the earth actually is in the hands of those to whom God has delegated it.

God does own the earth and continues to maintain the delicate balances of its functions and reveal His nature in it. Humanity, however, has been given the authority to affect or destroy even this aspect. God does not produce the consequences caused by pollution, wars and famine. It is not His will that people are abused, abandoned or mistreated. This is the will of humanity. Instead of doing what He wants, He waits patiently for us to discover the divine synergy found only in partnership with Him.

Stewardship
Since God created everything, it is in being yielded to Him that we discover the true purpose and design for all things. Humans are stewards rather than owners. Stewards are those who enjoy the benefits of use but are tasked also with the care and maintenance of things that they do not own. Jesus had a lot to say about stewardship in the New Testament. There are incredible promises for those who properly steward God's resources. Talents, time, money and even the kingdom of God has been placed in our hands to either use for His glory and our blessing or to misuse to our own peril, shame or even death.

God's goal with free will is to enable humanity to participate in relationship with Him on the earth. God's design and intentions for the earth are perfect. Instead of reigning on the earth without the knowledge of God's plan, Humanity has been given the awesome privilege to steward God's creation according to His design. God's participation is necessary because even with the best intentions not everything that humans do leads to life. Actions and attitudes that appear to be beneficial will result in destruction and even death if they are not according to God's divine design and purposes. (Proverbs 14:12).

In partnership with His people, God will gladly reveal the fullness of His love, purposes and blessing. His ways are higher than what we can imagine, but He will show us His ways and lead us in His paths (Isaiah 55:9). The invitation to partner with God is open!

Chapter Three

THE PRESENCE OF GOD

God is seated in the heavenlies. Jesus is at the right hand of the Father, but the residence of the Spirit of God is with humanity. The Bible, in the Old and New Testaments, describes the many ways that God, by His Spirit, interacts with humanity. For example, the Spirit of God "rushed upon" David (1 Samuel 16:13 ESV) and "clothed Gideon" (Judges 6:34 ESV), empowering and guiding both to purpose and victory.

The Spirit of God is the *presence of God* on the earth. It was the Spirit of God that overshadowed Mary so Jesus would be conceived. The Spirit of God descended upon Jesus like a dove at His baptism. Then the Spirit immediately led Jesus into the wilderness. Afterwards Jesus returned from the wilderness "in the power of the Spirit" to His life of supernatural ministry. It was the Spirit of God that initiated, empowered and guided the ministry of Jesus. (See Luke 1:35; 3:22 and 4:1,14 NIV.)

Theology exists among Christian communities to advance the idea that the Holy Spirit is a "force" *from* God rather than the full expression of God on the earth. While no orthodox believer would deny that the Holy Spirit is "the third Person of the Trinity," a reluctance exists among believers to fully embrace the *deity* of the presence of God among His people. This reluctance is due to the unique way that the Spirit of God often chooses to reveal Himself. The Spirit of God, as fully God, can only be fully revealed when those who seek Him are yielded in partnership with Him. The Spirit of God is sovereign and often moves and is manifest in ways that are unexpected and sometimes offensive when humans are not in partnership with Him. Some people find it difficult to accept that God can, without their permission, mysteriously do what He wants, even though the pattern of the Spirit working in this way is well documented in Scripture.

The presence of God is revealed on the earth in partnership with believers who seek to maintain an awareness of His presence and cultivate an environment where His is given room (not just permission) to move. Many believers, however, have not cultivated the disposition of humility that allows them to recognize the presence of God. They also are unable to yield to the presence of God because their theology (perception of God's personality or ability) does not permit them to do so. This is to their great loss.

Acceptance of and interaction with the Holy Spirit requires the discipline of "being yielded." Yielding to the Spirit (allowing God to guide and partnering with His will) is normative in the New Testament. Followers of Jesus are taught not to "quench" the Spirit (1 Thessalonians 5:19 NIV) or to grieve the Spirit (Ephesians 4:30). Instead, believers are instructed to walk by the Spirit (Galatians 5:16), be led by the Spirit (Romans 8:14), and live according to the Spirit (Romans 8:5).

The Bible reveals to us, by story and teaching, that the presence of God is active among us whether we see it or not! However, in order to experience and participate with the presence of God, we must cultivate and learn the discipline of being yielded to the presence of God among us. In chapters five through ten we will describe four practices that enable believers to interact and partner with the presence of God.

The primary way that God has chosen to reveal His presence on the earth is *in* and *through* His people! The proposal of God is that the "fullness of God" can exist within and among all those who are yielded to Him (Ephesians 3:19). This is God's primary plan to reveal His presence to the world. The intention of God to fill us with His presence is central to the prayer of Paul in Ephesians 3:

> *I pray that out of his glorious riches he may strengthen you with power through his Spirit in your inner being, so that Christ may dwell in your hearts through faith. And I pray that you, being rooted and established in love, may have power, together with all the Lord's holy people, to grasp how wide and long and high and deep is the love of Christ, and to know this love that surpasses knowledge—**that you may be filled to the measure of all the fullness of God**.* (Ephesians 3:16-19 NIV emphasis added)

Revealing the fullness of God by yielding to the presence of God was the pattern of Jesus. Jesus lived as a perfect man. He gave us an example of how to be yielded to God so as to allow the presence of God to be revealed to the world. Jesus did amazing miracles, signs and wonders, even though He told His disciples, "By myself, I can do nothing" (John 5:30 NIV). Jesus claimed that it was by the Spirit of God that He was able to do these things! (Matthew 12:28 NIV)

The Covenant
A covenant is an agreement between two parties. The word *covenant* comes from the Latin *con venire*, meaning "a coming together."[1] It is not a word in common usage, but it is still used in legal contexts to describe an agreement between two people—an agreement that includes promises, stipulations, privileges and responsibilities. A covenant is a way to establish a meaningful and lasting relationship between two parties.

The Bible is a record of God's covenant with His people. Participation and partnership with God is entirely optional. However, if people choose to live in partnership with God, then participation in His covenant is the only way. Participating with God, however, is a wonderful thing! The covenant that God makes with His people contains incredible promises and wonderful privileges. The covenant of God also contains conditions or stipulations.

Covenants are actually an essential part of *every* successful long-term relationship. Marriage is designed to be an amazing lifelong covenant between a man and a woman. In order for a marriage to succeed, it is essential that both parties know the expectations, responsibilities and privileges and mutually agree to them. Knowing the promises and privileges *as well as* conditions and stipulations of the marriage are critical. Knowing and following all aspects of the covenant creates a beautiful, lifelong experience for both partners. In the same way, God has proposed to live in covenant with humanity. Partnership in following the covenant is the only way for humanity to live in authentic relationship with God.

The covenant of Moses, often called the "old covenant," is the covenant that God instituted through Moses with His people about 1,500 years before Jesus came. Moses received the covenant from the presence of God on Mount Sinai. The covenant that Moses received included incredible promises and privileges as well as conditions and stipulations. The stipulations of the covenant called commandments were written down, and the priests and religious leaders were given the responsibility to teach them to the people. The people learned about what God expected from them, and when they heard and obeyed the covenant, the Lord blessed the people and fulfilled His wonderful promises.

According to the covenant, the presence of God existed in the Holy of Holies behind the thick veil of the temple, hidden from the view of all but the priests. Only priests were enabled according to the covenant to encounter, worship and minister to the presence of God.

The covenant of Moses was in effect right up until the time of Jesus. The history of God's relationship with His people under the old covenant is contained in the "Old Testament" of the Bible. When we study the Old Testament, we discover that it is full of instances where the presence of God was revealed to the *leaders* of the people. We discover that the Spirit of God would "come upon" leaders, judges, kings and prophets to give them supernatural power and to enable them to partner with God to properly lead the people.

The Bible tells us that Moses communed with the presence of God and talked with Him face to face "as a man speaks to his friend" (Exodus 33:11 NKJV). When governing the people became too much for

Moses to do by himself, he chose elders to assist him. They, like Moses, did not have the ability to govern the people without the power of God, so the Bible tells us that God took of the Spirit that was upon Moses and placed it upon the elders so that they could also "bear the burden" of leadership (Numbers 11:17 NKJV). The Spirit of God was given to Moses and the elders to *empower* them and give them *guidance* for leading the people of God.

This pattern of "presence before power" is important to notice as normal in Scripture. Starting with the story of Moses, the Old Testament reveals that the presence of God "came upon" a leader yielded to God, giving that person the supernatural ability to lead with wisdom and power. By being yielded to the Spirit, the presence of God enabled leaders to partner with God to lead with supernatural wisdom and power.

Gideon was a leader of the nation of Israel and lived about 300 years after Moses. He was not a formal leader. Instead, the Bible describes Gideon as a man who was afraid and disinterested in leadership (Judges 6:15,27 NIV). But the Bible also tells us that when Gideon responded in agreement to partner with God, the Spirit of God "came upon" Gideon so that he was supernaturally able to mobilize his people and lead them into victory against all their enemies (Judges 6:34 NKJV).

This transformation of Gideon and the battle that brought victory occurred in very unexpected ways. Rather than assailing Midian (the nation that was oppressing Israel) with as many warriors as possible, the Spirit of God led Gideon using a unique strategy. The Scripture records in Judges 7 that Gideon initially gathered 12,000 warriors from among the Israelites. However, when he gathered his army together, the Presence of the Lord directed Gideon to release all of the men who were "trembling with fear" and tell them to go home! The Bible tells us that 2,000 men simply left and went home! Following this reduction, God guided Gideon to use another selection strategy to further reduce his standing army from 10,000 to just 300 men! Just 300! But these 300 men and their unqualified commander were empowered and directed by the Spirit of God to defeat an army of 135,000 Midianites. This is one of many historical records of the way that God uses finite people and His supernatural power to reveal His glory and extend His Kingdom on the earth.

Of all the leaders in the Old Testament, David is the best example of ongoing transformation and partnership with the presence of God. David was a shepherd boy who loved to be alone with God (Psalm 16:11). David lived 250 years after Gideon and was the second king of Israel (around 1000 B.C.E). When David was young, the prophet Samuel was led by the Spirit of God to visit the home of his father Jesse. First Samuel 16 describes his mission. Samuel had been commissioned by the presence of God to find and then to anoint the next king of Israel. The story of what happened at this meeting is astonishing! After insisting that Jesse bring all of his sons before him one at a time, Samuel did not choose *any of them*. Instead, he asked, "'Are these all the sons that you have?' 'There is still the youngest,' Jesse answered. 'He is tending the sheep'" (verse 11). In response, Samuel stated that he would not sit down until David was brought before him. David was quickly retrieved from his post in the fields with the sheep. When Samuel saw him, he was immediately instructed by the Spirit to anoint him as king of Israel.

So Samuel took the horn of oil and anointed him in the presence of his brothers, and from that day on the Spirit of the LORD came powerfully upon David.... (1 Samuel 16:13 NIV)

The Scripture declared that the presence of God *came powerfully upon* David! This event took place nearly fifteen years before David became king of Israel! However, from the moment of his anointing going forward, the Scriptures reveal that David cultivated a passion and a yielded heart for the presence of God. This partnership with God gave him a singular place in history. The Psalms written by David are familiar references to the presence of God and reveal that David continuously cultivated an intimate, "face to face" relationship like the one Moses experienced. When caught in the sin of adultery, one of David's primary concerns is the loss of his relationship with the presence God! David wrote, "Do not cast me from your presence or take your Holy Spirit from me" (Psalm 51:11 NIV). Because David loved to be in the presence of God, according to Psalm 61:4, he did not want anything to become a barrier. As a musician, David used worship as a primary way of expressing his heart and attracting the presence of God. In worship and partnership with the presence of God, David was empowered with joy, guidance and the strength he needed to lead his people (Psalm 16:11; 22:19).

When David finally became king, one of his primary tasks was to commission instrumentalists and singers to minister to the presence of the Lord before the ark of the covenant (1 Chronicles 16:4,7,37-40). So passionate was the heart of David for intimacy with the presence of God that he is known in the Old and New Testaments as "a man after [God's] own heart" (1 Samuel 13:14 NKJV).

Not only did the presence of God guide and empower the judges and kings, but His presence also empowered the prophets of the old covenant. Isaiah was a prophet to the people of Israel around 730 B.C.E. He also experienced a relationship with the Spirit of God and wrote often about it. He described himself as a messenger sent from the Lord and "endowed with his Spirit" (Isaiah 48:16 NIV).

> *The Spirit of the Sovereign LORD is on me, because the LORD has anointed me to proclaim good news to the poor. He has sent me to bind up the brokenhearted, to proclaim freedom for the captives and release from darkness for the prisoners, to proclaim the year of the LORD's favor and the day of vengeance of our God, to comfort all who mourn. (Isaiah 61:1-2 NIV)*

This is the passage that Jesus read in the synagogue just after He was baptized! The Spirit of the Lord was upon Jesus! His mission was to proclaim good news, free captives and deliver those who were imprisoned in darkness. This was Jesus's mission statement!

Instead of continuing to reveal His purposes and presence through prophets, priests and kings, it was God's plan to restore His desire for presence-based community through Jesus. It was through Jesus that an entirely new covenant – a presence-based community- would be established!

Chapter Four

PRESENCE-BASED COMMUNITY

God's plan has always been to live in face-to-face community with His people. He established Eden as the original place of encounter with Adam. In Eden, God lived in unmitigated connection and involvement with His people. From the time of Moses until John the Baptist, the people of God were dependent on the ministry of leaders who met with God face to face. These priests, prophets and kings met with God in order to reveal the plans and purposes of God to the people.

One hundred and fifty years before Jesus was born, the prophet Jeremiah announced God's plan for establishing a new covenant:

> *"The day is coming," says the LORD, "when I will make a new covenant with the people of Israel and Judah. **This covenant will not be like the one I made with their ancestors** when I took them by the hand and brought them out of the land of Egypt. They broke that covenant, though I loved them as a husband loves his wife," says the LORD. "But **this is the new covenant I will make** with the people of Israel after those days," says the LORD. "I will*

put my instructions deep within them, and I will write them on their hearts. I will be their God, and they will be my people. And they will not need to teach their neighbors, nor will they need to teach their relatives, saying, 'You should know the LORD.' For everyone, from the least to the greatest, will know me already," says the LORD. "And I will forgive their wickedness, and I will never again remember their sins." (Jeremiah 31:31-34 NLT, emphasis added)

Jeremiah declared that the *new* covenant would be quite different from the old one in numerous ways. Instead of God communicating with His people through their leaders and giving them access to His precepts and instructions from written sources alone, God would now write His precepts and instructions *within* each person. Instead of reliance on the teaching of others, *everyone* would know Him, from those who are unlearned and illiterate (the least) to those who are highly educated (the greatest).

One can only imagine the questions that this prophecy created. How can everyone know God without being taught? How will God reveal His instructions to each person? What will the role of priests and teachers be if everyone can hear God directly? Even more amazing is the prophecy of Joel who lived 750 years before Jesus. Joel declared:

*And it shall come to pass afterward that **I will pour out My Spirit on all flesh**; your sons and your daughters shall **prophesy**, your old men shall dream_**dreams**, your young men shall see **visions**. And also on My menservants and on My maidservants I will pour out My Spirit in those days.* (Joel 2:28-29 NKJV, emphasis added)

If we are to understand that this passage is about the new covenant (as most scholars do), then it seems that the mechanism of God's plan is that the Spirit of God will be "poured out" on all believers just like God did with Moses, Gideon and David. This outpouring would be not just on men (as He had in the past), but on women, too! Men and women would not only *experience* the presence of the Lord, but they also would prophesy and have dreams like the prophets did in the old covenant. No longer would God reveal His mysteries just to prophets, but also to all men and women, young and old, illiterate and learned!

How would the people of this presence-based community live together and operate in harmony if everyone has this capacity? The answer can be discovered in the *teaching* and *example* of Jesus and the early Church.

The Presence of God in the New Covenant

Jesus lived a life that was entirely yielded in relationship to the presence of God. He often woke up before daybreak to commune with God (Mark 1:35). He often stayed up all night to pray (Luke 6:12). Luke's Gospel simply states that "Jesus often withdrew to lonely places and prayed" (Luke 5:16 NIV). The life of Jesus flowed out of intimacy with the presence of God; all that He said and did was watered by the stream of living water that flowed within Him.

Jesus never resisted the presence of God. He never grieved the presence of God or quenched the Spirit. Instead of doing what He thought was best, Jesus told them, "...the Son can do nothing by himself; he can do only what he sees his Father doing..." (John 5:19 NIV). To those who questioned His teaching, He replied, "My teaching is not my own" and "I am telling you what I have seen in the Father's presence" (John 7:16; 8:38 NIV). Jesus reflected the full spectrum of the presence of God, not because of His divine nature but because of His intimate connection and communication with the presence of God. His was a lifestyle of listening and responding and serving others in yielded participation with the presence of God.

When His disciples asked Him to tell them who God was, Jesus shocked them all by saying, "Anyone who has seen me has seen the Father" (John 14:9 NIV). Jesus had been so saturated in the presence of God that His attitudes, thoughts and even His physical presence had been transformed. His reflection of the nature of God was so pure and real that His very presence reflected the presence of God on the earth!

The living presence of God was inside of Jesus. The presence of God within Him truly was a river of living water. During the last and greatest day of the yearly Feast of Tabernacles in the great outer court of Herod's temple, all the people of Israel would gather for a special libation ceremony called "Simchat Beit Hashoavah." It was a worship celebration to affirm God as the source of rain for drinking water and for producing crops on the earth. During this ceremony, it was the custom of the priests to fill a golden vessel with the water from the pool of Siloam. They would carry this water up to the temple and then pour the water so that it flowed over the altar. It was during this event that Jesus gave an extraordinary invitation to the multitude of people gathered there:[1]

> ...*Jesus stood and said in a loud voice,* **"Let anyone who is thirsty come to me and drink.** *Whoever believes in me, as Scripture has said,* **rivers of living water will flow from within them." By this he meant the Spirit, whom those who believed in him were later to receive.** *Up to that time the Spirit had not been given, since Jesus had not yet been glorified.* (John 7:37-39 NIV, emphasis added)

The context for Jesus's great invitation is amazing! In the midst of recognizing God's provision of water for the thirst of a nation, Jesus was inviting all members of the old covenant to come to *Him* and receive water that would enable "rivers of *living* water" to flow from within them. Of course, Jesus was inviting them to receive the Spirit of God -the presence of God- that would be poured out at Pentecost. Jesus, the Author of the new covenant, not only taught and demonstrated a life of intimacy with the Spirit of God, but also came to make intimacy with the Spirit of God available to everyone!

There was one day, however, that Jesus experienced complete separation from the presence of God. The writers of the Gospels report that on the day when Jesus was crucified, it became as dark as night in the middle of the day. In the midst of this darkness, Jesus shouted, "My God, my God, why have you forsaken me?" (Matthew 27:46 NIV). The agony of Jesus on the cross was not caused by the betrayal of His closest friends.

It was not the rejection and sentence of death placed upon Him by the religious leaders. It was not the torture inflicted on Him by the Roman government. The anguished cry of Jesus was caused by the dark separation that occurred when God placed the sin of all humanity upon Him. Until that moment, Jesus lived in unbroken communion with God.

> *"He himself bore our sins" in his body on the cross, so that we might die to sins and live for righteousness; "by his wounds you have been healed."* (1 Peter 2:24 NIV)

At the moment of Jesus's death, something truly astonishing happened:

> *And when Jesus had cried out again in a loud voice, he gave up his spirit. At that moment **the curtain of the temple was torn in two from top to bottom**....* (Matthew 27:50-51 NIV)

The veil in the temple that had separated the people from the presence of God in the Holy of Holies was torn from *top* to *bottom*. Access to the presence of God was open! The presence of God was no longer limited to the Holy of Holies and dependent on human mediators. The veil that had separated God from humanity for nearly 1,600 years was opened! The covenant of Moses had been fulfilled. The veil was removed so that, instead of just the priests, and just as Jeremiah had prophesied, the new covenant would not be like the old, instead, "They will all know me, from the least of them to the greatest" (Jeremiah 31:34 NIV).

In the dark days following Jesus's crucifixion, the disciples were full of fear. Judas committed suicide. Peter, whom Jesus had named "the rock," had publicly denied that he even knew who Jesus was! The disciples of Jesus were being hunted by the religious leaders. It was a mess! The whole situation just seemed like a total failure. The disciples were full of shame, huddled together like refugees in their homes, meeting in secret, fearful of being arrested.

Where was the power now? Why didn't the disciples know what to do? Was their problem a lack of knowledge? They were with Jesus for nearly three years. He had taught them everything about the Kingdom of God and their place in it, but where was that knowledge now? Was it more knowledge that was needed? Everything was so clear when Jesus was with them. Now Jesus was gone, and so was the power of God. The disciples had to face the facts: without Jesus they truly were powerless; even worse, they were afraid and full of shame. Without the presence of Jesus with them, they felt like orphans!

When Jesus was raised from the dead, the disciples saw the empty tomb and the folded graveclothes, but they still did not understand what was going on! (John 20:1-9; Luke 24:12). It was not until they had gathered in Jerusalem that Jesus came and stood among them. They were overjoyed and began to understand why Jesus died and what His resurrection meant! They *began* to believe that what Jesus had told them was true, and they began to have faith in what Jesus told them no matter what the situation was around them. Over a period of forty days, Jesus met with His disciples to encourage them. During these encounters, Jesus "opened their minds" by explaining the prophecies about Him and the meaning of His death and resurrection (Luke 24:44-45). But still they had no power and they still did not know what to do!

On one occasion when Jesus was with them, He told them to gather in "Jerusalem until you are endued with power from on high" (Luke 24:49 NKJV). On another occasion He told them what to do: "*wait* for the gift my Father promised" (Acts 1:4 NIV), and then He described what would happen. He said, "John baptized with water, but in a few days you will be baptized with the Holy Spirit" (Acts 1:5 NIV). During this preparation period of forty days, Jesus met with His disciples to open their minds and encourage them about what the new covenant. Finally, forty days after His last supper with the disciples, Jesus asked them to gather with Him on a mountain near Galilee. At this last gathering, Jesus blessed them and then gave them specific instructions:

> …"*All authority has been given to Me in heaven and on earth. Go therefore and* **make disciples** *of all the nations,* **baptizing them** *in the name of the Father and of the Son and of the Holy Spirit,* **teaching them** *to observe all things that I have commanded you; and lo,* **I am with you always,** *even to the end of the age."* *Amen.* (Matthew 28:18-20 NKJV)

The followers of Jesus were commissioned to baptize, teach and disciple others just as they had been discipled by Jesus! Instead of being intermediaries of God's presence, teaching others about "how to know the Lord," new believers would follow in the steps of the twelve (now called *apostles*, meaning "sent ones"). New believers would walk alongside of the disciples of Jesus, being mentored by them, learning how to hear and respond to Jesus as they did. They would be equipped by the disciples to learn how to minister to others and live in community just like Jesus and His disciples did.

In obedience to Jesus, the disciples gathered in Jerusalem along with others, both men and women, until 120 were gathered in an upper room. Out of obedience to the instructions of Jesus, they gathered for ten days! Did you know that the events of Pentecost were preceded by 10 days of prayer? During this time, they followed the practices that Jesus taught them. They did as he commanded by "waiting" on God in prayer. The Bible describes it this way:

> *These all continued **with one accord in prayer and supplication**, with the women and Mary the mother of Jesus, and with His brothers.* (Acts 1:14 NKJV)

Instead of gathering to discuss the teachings of Jesus, the disciples met with the core group of Jesus's followers to wait "with one accord in prayer and supplication."

The Birth of Presence-Based Community

The first gathering of the Church was a prayer meeting. The goal of this meeting was waiting for an *encounter* with God, gathering in expectation and yieldedness to the presence of the Lord. Notice that the manner of praying is described as "with one accord." This is of immense importance. These periods of prayer were not about praying silently and individually. Praying "in one accord" simply means that they prayed with one heart and mind. It is a description of passionate, united prayer. Can you imagine the sight—a gathering of all the people who loved Jesus pouring out their hearts in prayer, waiting in expectancy and meeting for ten days straight? No one knows exactly what the "program" was for these meetings, but we do know that if the prayer was done according to the example of Jesus, then they must have prayed both day and night. Perhaps some of them would go home to rest or eat. Perhaps they fasted. We only know that after ten days...

> *When the Day of Pentecost had fully come, **they were all with one accord** in one place. And suddenly there came a sound from heaven, as of a rushing mighty wind, and it filled the whole house where they were sitting. Then there appeared to them divided tongues, as of fire, and one sat upon each of them. **And they were all filled with the Holy Spirit** and began to speak with other tongues, as the Spirit gave them utterance.* (Acts 2:1-4 NKJV)

The Church was birthed at Pentecost! Pentecost was not an optional "experience" after salvation for the followers of Jesus. Before the Spirit of God was given as Jesus promised, there was no Church. After Pentecost, the promised Counselor had come, and as Jesus had promised, the presence of God would be among them to guide them and empower them just like Jesus did when He was with them!

In the same way that the presence of God came upon Moses, Gideon, David and Jesus, the presence of God now invaded the lives of all those who met in yielded expectation. Now the followers of Jesus were yielded partners with the presence of God who would guide and enable them to live supernatural lives full of purpose and power!

Before Pentecost, the disciples were powerless, fearful and unable to imagine what the future held for them. After Pentecost, they were a purposeful and powerful presence-based community, both men and women, young and old, slave and free, living in and revealing the love and presence of God. The Book of Acts records the extraordinary nature of the early Church. They lived in humility, holiness and in freedom from the tyranny of sin because of the presence of God among them.

The Church after Pentecost consisted of people who were discipled in relationship by the apostles. Because of the love that the presence of God was giving them, they selflessly cared for one another. Those who had extra unselfishly shared with those in need so that there was no needy among them (Acts 4:34).

The early Church continued the discipleship pattern of Jesus by regularly gathering in their homes and in large public places for authentic, corporate worship and passionate, united prayer. As a result, all the believers were "filled with awe," because they experienced the revelation of God's power in supernatural signs and wonders (Acts 2:43 NIV). Above all, the society of believers cared deeply and sacrificially for one another. Because of this, the Lord "added to their number daily those who were being saved" (Acts 2:47 NIV).

The new covenant community that Jesus birthed was not based on obeying laws, working harder or even knowing more. The love of God was multiplied in hearts and minds because of connection to Jesus and one another! Instead of growing in personal ability, true followers of Jesus selflessly served others with powerful and purposeful lives out of yieldedness to the presence of God. They discovered that following in the steps of Jesus was not complicated, but neither was it easy. Jesus described it this way:

Then he said to them all: "Whoever wants to be my disciple must deny themselves and take up their cross daily and follow me. For whoever wants to save their life will lose it, but whoever loses their life for me will save it." (Luke 9:23-24 NIV)

Preparation for a life in relationship with God and others is not accomplished by working harder. The new covenant is accomplished by death to self and living in yieldedness to God and in service to others. No other kind of lifestyle is worth living! Instead of doing what each believer wants to do or trying to figure out what God wants, the new covenant is accomplished by in yielded communion with the Spirit in order to be "taught by God." Instead of living in isolation, each yielded believer is loved and cared for by the Spirit of God working through the spirit led ministry of other believers! Jesus is the supreme example for this journey. He did not fight to be God. He knew who He was; instead, He laid down His rights, picked up His cross and responded in yielded obedience to God as an example for us. In response to His yieldedness, God raised Him up and gave Him great honor. (See Philippians 2:1-11.) Then Jesus commissioned His disciples to do the same as He had done—to disciple others by walking alongside them to serve and care for them. The apostle John described it this way: "Love has been perfected among us...because as He is, so are we in this world" (1 John 4:17 NKJV).

FOUR PRINCIPLES FOR PRESENCE-BASED COMMUNITY

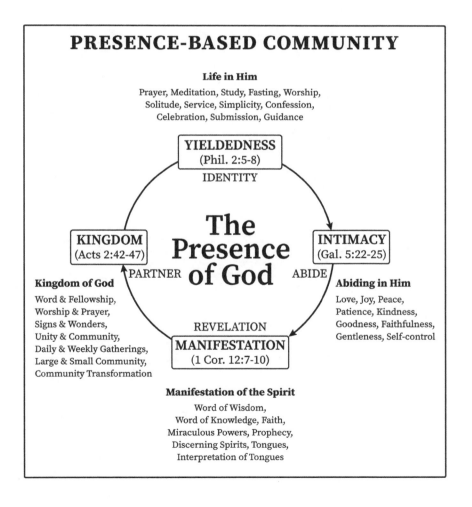

PRESENCE-BASED COMMUNITY

Life in Him

Prayer, Meditation, Study, Fasting, Worship,
Solitude, Service, Simplicity, Confession,
Celebration, Submission, Guidance

YIELDEDNESS
(Phil. 2:5-8)

IDENTITY

KINGDOM
(Acts 2:42-47)

The Presence of God

INTIMACY
(Gal. 5:22-25)

PARTNER   ABIDE

Kingdom of God

Word & Fellowship,
Worship & Prayer,
Signs & Wonders,
Unity & Community,
Daily & Weekly Gatherings,
Large & Small Community,
Community Transformation

REVELATION

MANIFESTATION
(1 Cor. 12:7-10)

Abiding in Him

Love, Joy, Peace,
Patience, Kindness,
Goodness, Faithfulness,
Gentleness, Self-control

Manifestation of the Spirit

Word of Wisdom,
Word of Knowledge, Faith,
Miraculous Powers, Prophecy,
Discerning Spirits, Tongues,
Interpretation of Tongues

Section TWO

PRACTICES OF PRESENCE-BASED COMMUNITY

Chapter Five
THE GATEWAY PRINCIPLE

The Bible tells us that some people were *able* to accept Jesus and others were *unable* to accept Jesus when He came. Specifically, some were *able to accept* that Jesus was presenting "God's way" while others were unable and so rejected what Jesus was saying.

> *All the people, even the tax collectors, when they heard Jesus' words, **acknowledged that God's way was right**, because **they had been baptized** by John. But the Pharisees and the experts in the law **rejected God's purpose for themselves**, because **they had not been baptized** by John.* (Luke 7:29-30 NIV, emphasis added)

The meaning of this passage in Luke 7 is quite insightful. Why was the baptism of John so important? What was it about baptism that made people more receptive to the ministry of Jesus?

Baptism was not unknown among the people of Jesus's day. The priests in the temple and various other sectarian groups such as the Essenes practiced it.[1] Being publicly immersed in water usually signified a a desire to be cleansed from sin. It was a public event that indicated to all present that the one being baptized wished to be set apart to God. But John's invitation was for more than just a spiritual wash:

> *In those days John the Baptist came preaching in the wilderness of Judea, and saying,* **"Repent, for the kingdom of heaven is at hand!"** *For this is he who was spoken of by the prophet Isaiah, saying: "The voice of one crying in the wilderness: 'Prepare the way of the LORD; make His paths straight.'"* (Matthew 3:1-3 NKJV)

John's message was a clarion call for *repentance* in preparation for the coming reign of God! People coming to John to be baptized were not responding only to be cleansed from sin; rather, it was their intention to be prepared for the imminent coming of God's Kingdom among them! Being submersed in the waters signified repentance from sin *and* preparedness for what God was about to do! It was an public act of humility and openness to God! The spiritual significance of submitting to baptism as an expression of *humility* toward God cannot be underestimated. Baptism was so important as a preparation for the ministry of Jesus that when John was imprisoned, Jesus and His disciples continued to baptize! John's Gospel actually records that Jesus's disciples baptized *more* people than John (John 4:1-2)!

The Bible says that John called out to everyone, "Prepare the way of the Lord, Make straight paths for Him!" (Matthew 3:3 NIV). John specifically challenged the religious leaders, warning them to turn away from pride and toward God in humility (Matthew 3:7). Some did respond, but most did not! John's call for baptism was a challenge to everyone who heard him. They were challenged to "repent," to turn away from sin and self in order to be *yielded* and ready for the soon-coming reign of God!

Jesus called John the greatest prophet who ever lived (Luke 7:28 NKJV)! For most of my life, I wondered why Jesus would express such value for John's ministry. Of course, John was a faithful witness, but his ministry seemed insignificant! He performed no miracles and did not prophesy in great oracles like Isaiah and Jeremiah! In fact, John seemed to fade in his faith when he was placed in prison. Even though he recognized Jesus at His baptism (Mathew 3:13-15), John sent his disciples from his prison cell to ask Jesus, "Are you the one who is to come, or should we expect someone else?" (Luke 7:19). How can John be the greatest prophet?

I finally realized that John's ministry was that of a forerunner. His work was to "prepare a way" for the Son of God! John was the greatest, not because of *who* he was, but because of what he did! His ministry was critical to the success of Jesus's ministry. By calling the people to repent, he gave them an opportunity to become yielded and prepared. The people who came to him and yielded their hearts to God by being baptized were prepared for the presence-based ministry of Jesus. Those who had been baptized by John were living in expectation of a move of God and therefore could understand and accept who Jesus was and what Jesus was teaching! Those who did not repent were not prepared because they had not yielded to God in preparation for the ministry of Jesus. John was not just a prophet; he was a herald and a forerunner for the new covenant prophesied by Malachi:

> *Behold, I send My messenger,* **and he will prepare the way before Me**. *And the Lord, whom you seek, will suddenly come to His temple, even* **the Messenger of the covenant, in whom you delight**... (Malachi 3:1 NKJV, emphasis added)

For an entire year, my quiet time seemed to be centered on this phenomenon in the ministry of John. I could not stop thinking about the work of John as a *forerunner* to Jesus and how being yielded was so important for those who accepted Jesus's ministry Why would this condition of "being yielded" be so necessary just to even *recognize* who Jesus was?

Yieldedness

I realized that maintaining a yielded heart toward God is *a gateway principle* contained in the new covenant. Not only was being yielded to God necessary in order for the people to hear and accept Jesus when He came, it continues to be necessary in order for all people in all times in order to be prepared to see, hear and respond to presence of God.

Jesus teachings about the condition of being humble, yielded and prepared for God are quite extensive. Often Jesus would conclude His teaching by saying, "Whoever has ears to hear, let them hear" (Mark 4:9; Luke 8:8 NIV). When asked by His disciples why he spoke to the people in parables He responded:

> *The disciples came to Him and asked, "Why do you speak to the people in parables?" He replied, "Because the knowledge of the secrets of the kingdom of heaven **has been given to you, but not to them**. Whoever has will be given more, and they will have an abundance. Whoever does not have, even what they have will be taken from them. This is why I speak to them in parables: Though seeing, they do not see; though hearing, they do not hear or understand." (Matthew 13:10-13 NIV, emphasis added)*

Why would the knowledge of the Kingdom of God be "given" to some but not others? What is Jesus talking about when He says that "Whoever has will be given more... Whoever does not have, even what they have will be taken away from them..." It seems unfair that some people who have more would be given an abundance and others who have very little would be plundered of what they have! What is the meaning of Jesus teaching here?

It is essential to note that this statement follows the parable of the sower. In this parable, Jesus described what is necessary for the Word of God (the seed) to take root in the hearts of people (the soil). In the parable, a sower is planting his seed by casting it over his field. Some of the seed lands on soil that is *hard and unable to receive* the seed: "the path." Some of the seed lands on soil that is *cultivated and able to receive* the seed: "good soil" (Matthew 13:18-23). The seed that landed on hard, unyielding soil did not take root, but was immediately stolen away! But the seed that landed in soil that had been yielded to the plow was able to take root and produce a bountiful crop! In essence, the key to growth in the Kingdom of God is not is not in the viability of the Word of God, but in the receptivity of the hearts into which it is sown. Hearts that are hard cannot receive the Word of God but must instead be yielded in order for the Word of God to take root and grow. This condition of being yielded is necessary before the Word of God can even begin to take root! Yieldedness—a condition of the heart—is a necessary condition in order to hear and receive the Word of God!

In seminary I encountered the concept of *yieldedness* for the first time. It was written in another language. *Gellasenheit* was a word used by the early Anabaptists. It describes an attitude, a discipline of "yieldedness." Anabaptism grew out of a spiritual awakening that took place in Germany and Switzerland in the 1520s just prior to the Reformation. The early Anabaptists practiced and taught adult baptism in opposition to infant baptism practices of the Roman Catholics. They practiced *gellassenheit* as a spiritual discipline and considered it essential for true Christian community.[2] According to the Anabaptists, *gellassenheit* is a disposition of love in "being yielded inwardly to the Spirit of God and outwardly to the community of believers." They taught that *gellassenheit* was fully demonstrated by the disposition of Jesus toward God and others.[3] A disposition of yieldedness is best expressed by the words of Jesus, who said, "*not my will, but thine be done*" in relationship with God and "*I have not come to be served but to serve*" in relationship with others.

Although the word *yieldedness* is not in the dictionary, I began to use the word. Yieldedness seems to be the best word to describe the gateway principle to presence-based community in the Bible. Once I began to search the Scriptures, I noticed that cultivation of yieldedness is found everywhere and is *essential*, even foundational, to every aspect of the new covenant both as it relates to a relationship with God and in relationship toward others.

Jesus used this example to explain the principle to His disciples: He told them that unless they "become [yielded] like little children," they would "never enter the kingdom of heaven" (Matthew 18:3 NIV). He described how this necessary attitude was like a kernel of wheat that dies and is planted in the ground. He taught them that until the seed was yielded, it could not produce fruit (John 12:24). Then He spoke clearly:

> *Anyone who loves their life will lose it, while anyone who hates their life in this world will keep it for eternal life.* (John 12:25 NIV)

Jesus taught that yieldedness to God is the key for *entry* to the Kingdom of God. Yieldedness to God is the key for *fruitfulness* in the Kingdom of God and yieldedness is necessary for *eternal life* in the Kingdom of God. Although I had heard these Scriptures my entire life, I really did not understand their implications. I knew that humility and surrender were necessary for salvation! But I certainly did not understand that, to be a true follower of Jesus, I would literally need to "lay down my life" in yielded surrender as an ongoing spiritual discipline.

I am not the only one. I believe that a disposition of entitlement and consumerism persists in nearly all of the Church in the West. Entitlement is a prevailing attitude within of our culture. It is this attitude of entitlement that prohibits comfortable believers from yielding to anything. Our national attitude related to "life, liberty and the pursuit of happiness" causes us to refrain from involvement in any situation where we are not in charge. People with an entitled mindset cannot understand presence-based community, much less participate in it because it makes no sense to "die to self," especially as the first order of business.

The gateway principle for presence-based community is yieldedness to God. This is what Jesus taught, demonstrated and gave to the Church as His inheritance. The problem for most people in Western culture who encounter the principle of yieldedness is that they don't understand what it means. Most have never truly been *yielded* to anything or anybody!

The Sovereignty of God

The key to understanding yieldedness is understanding sovereignty. Sovereigns answer to no one. Sovereigns do not reign by consent of those governed. Sovereigns do whatever they please! Western minds recoil at the idea of sovereignty. We can't imagine being completely yielded and obedient to someone who can do and say what they please, even if that person is the Creator God who is full of love and can do no wrong!

In Western civilizations, we don't have a place in our imagination for the correct way to respond to a sovereign. With this in mind, it became clear to me that I had no idea what I was saying when I said, "Jesus Christ is Lord." I had no grid for understanding yieldedness. I didn't know that the only correct way to respond to Jesus as Lord was with a lifestyle of yieldedness. I also didn't know that living in yieldedness to God would allow me to live in the fullness and purpose that I was created for! Being yielded to the creator allows me to partner with a loving God to experience abundant life. (John 10:10)

If the presence-based community that Jesus created with His disciples is to be perpetuated on the earth today, the practices of the Church must shift in emphasis from Jesus as teacher to Jesus as Lord. I began to see that I had spent so much of my life learning *about* Jesus that I did not know truly know Him. I had been searching the Scriptures to find life, but like the Pharisees, I had failed to come to Him (seek His face) to understand who He really is.

> **You search the Scriptures**, *for in them you think you have eternal life; and these are they which testify of Me.* **But you are not willing to come to Me that you may have life**. (John 5:39-40 NKJV emphasis added)

The Church must make a radical shift in its approach to Jesus in this regard. Instead of giving our primary energies to learning *about* Him, we need to shift our primary attention to learning *from* Him. Bible study truly is essential as a primary devotion of the Church listed in Acts 2:42, but our life is not based on a knowledge of the Scriptures. Instead, abundant life is experienced in the knowledge of God!

The gateway principle of yieldedness is also present in the example of all the patriarchs. Abraham lived in yielded surrender to God, who led him daily. Moses also lived in yieldedness to God. In face to face communion, he did only as he was directed. David was a shepherd boy who submitted his life to God. All of these heroes of faith lived in yielded relationship with God, who led them sovereignly to see the purposes, love and power of God revealed on the earth.

Jesus taught, "He who is greatest among you shall be your servant" (Matthew 23:11 NKJV). In Jesus's Sermon on the Mount, the key to the Kingdom is yieldedness: "Blessed are the poor in spirit, for theirs is the kingdom of heaven" (Matthew 5:3 NKJV). The Greek word for "poor" in this verse means "crouching."[4] In essence, the reign of God is reserved for those who are crouching or yielded rather than proud in spirit.

Jesus is the supreme example of a lifestyle of yieldedness to God. Paul described this gateway attitude as being the "mind" of Jesus. He wrote:

> Let this mind be in you which was also in Christ Jesus, who, being in the form of God, did not consider it robbery to be equal with God, **but made Himself of no reputation**, taking the form of a bondservant, and coming in the likeness of men. And being found in appearance as a man, **He humbled Himself and became obedient to the point of death**, even the death of the cross. (Philippians 2:5-8 NKJV, emphasis added)

Paul also described the results of Jesus's yieldedness to God.

> **Therefore God also has highly exalted Him** and given Him the name which is above every name, that at the name of Jesus every knee should bow, of those in heaven, and of those on earth, and of those under the earth, and that every tongue should confess that Jesus Christ is Lord, to the glory of God the Father. (Philippians 2:9-11 NKJV, emphasis added)

Yieldedness does not *end* in misery! Because of His yieldedness to God, Jesus conquered death and now sits exalted in the heavenlies. Now He has given us a path to follow!

The path of yieldedness is not directed by those who walk on it. Instead of human strength being a primary requirement, God has made human weakness a prerequisite. The discipline of humbleness has always been a gateway to blessing. God has always resisted the proud and given grace to the humble (Proverbs 3:34; James 4:6). The example of Jesus makes it clear that the mind of Christ was yielded, so we, too, must live this way. In fact, Jesus declared that it was absolutely necessary to the new covenant.

The Cross

The cross of Jesus is the starting place for everything! Because of His great love for us and the Father, Jesus laid down His life and made a way for us by His shed blood on the cross. The cross of Jesus is also the starting place for presence-based community. We must follow the path that Jesus laid out for the disciples:

> *Then he said to them all: "Whoever wants to be my disciple must deny themselves and take up their cross daily and follow me."* (Luke 9:23 NIV)

Western Christians tend to believe that salvation is the first step to becoming a follower of Christ. We are taught that we must "accept Jesus" so we can have eternal life. Jesus did not invite His disciples to "accept Him." Instead, He told them, "You cannot be My disciple unless you lay down your life" (Matthew 16:24, Luke 9:23). Instead of inviting people to accept Jesus, we must present them with the real opportunity to "give their lives to" Jesus. Yieldedness is the *first* step on the journey and in *every* step thereafter! The Scriptures confirm that we are saved when we call upon His name (Romans 10:13), but we only experience the life of God in us when we live in yieldedness to Him as Lord!

The cross was not just an historic event. It represents a pattern that determines the path of all believers.

> *Now if we died with Christ, we believe that we will also live with him. For we know that since Christ was raised from the dead, he cannot die again; death no longer has mastery over him. The death he died, he died to sin once for all; but the life he*

lives, he lives to God. ***In the same way, count yourselves dead to sin but alive to God in Christ Jesus.*** (Romans 6:8-11 NIV, emphasis added)

In yieldedness we have the privelage and challenge of to picking up our cross, and "living to God." In doing this we become dead to sin (Romans 8:13-14). Dying to self does not mean that we are without worth; instead, dying to self allows us to be raised from the dead! Dying to self allows us to be dead to sin and alive to God. Yieldedness is not only the way to be saved. The gateway principle is necessary for every aspect of the Christian life.

Yieldedness to God is the way we participate in the Kingdom. As we yield to God as Jesus did, we live in the power of God as Jesus did. As we die to self, we live more fully in the life of God. As we choose to walk in brokenness, we are continually being renewed. As we resist the temptation to live for ourselves and learn to live in communion with the presence of God, we reveal His power and His purposes to those around us.

We enter into partnership with Jesus by denying self and living for God. Paul described the spiritual physics involved: "This is a faithful saying: For if we died with Him, we shall also live with Him" (2 Timothy 2:11 NKJV). But Paul also warned, "...If we disown him, he will also disown us" (2 Timothy 2:12 NIV).

Every human has a choice, but the choice is not to "accept Jesus." It is a choice to either live for self (in separation from God) or to live in yieldedness to Him to discover His abundant life. The cross of Jesus means that we participate by yieldedness to God, by surrender, in order to be transformed!

Yieldedness in Community

The cross of Jesus demonstrates that yieldedness to God results in self-less love for others. "God so loved the world that he *gave*" Jesus to die on the cross (John 3:16 NIV, emphasis added). It was the sovereignty of God that led Jesus to give His life as a ransom for the whole world. But it was not only the will of God that led Jesus to die. Because of yieldedness to God, Jesus Himself was full of love for the world. John

the Apostle described how yieldedness in relationship with God results in selfless love for others:

> *This is how we know what love is:* **Jesus Christ laid down his**
> **life for us.** *And* **we ought to lay down our lives for our brothers**
> **and sisters.** *If anyone has material possessions and sees a brother*
> *or sister in need but has no pity on them,* **how can the love of**
> **God be in that person?** *Dear children, let us not love with words*
> *or speech but with actions and in truth.* (1 John 3:16-18 NIV,
> emphasis added)

A lifestyle of yieldedness to God also is a lifestyle of yieldedness
to "lay down our lives" for others. John claimed that selfless love for
others is evidence that God's love is within us! In fact, John continued to reveal that selfless love for others is the evidence that God
lives within us!

> *Dear friends, since God so loved us, we also ought to love one*
> *another. No one has ever seen God;* **but if we love one another,**
> **God lives in us and his love is made complete in us.** *This is how*
> *we know that we live in him and he in us: He has given us of his*
> *Spirit.* (1 John 4:11-13 NIV, emphasis added)

Loving others is a behavior that will be present if God lives in us!
Allowing God's love to be made "complete" in our lives means yieldedness to the presence of God in order to serve one another.

The Western Church struggles with selfless love. Most believers
understand that we are called to love one another, but "laying down
our lives" for one another seems to be dependent on our own desire
and comfort level rather than the cross of Jesus. Instead of selfless love
being one of the characteristics of the Western Church, many members feel isolated and unattached. Instead of gathering to express love
to God and express love and care for others, the purpose for gathering
often is to learn about God and receive care from church leaders.

A presence-based community consists of those who selflessly
love one another because of yieldedness to the powerful love of God

within them. They become instruments of God's love to others. A presence-based community lives according to the example of Jesus, who said:

> ...*whoever wants to become great among you must be your servant, and whoever wants to be first must be your slave—just as the Son of Man did not come to be served, but to serve, and to give his life as a ransom for many.* (Matthew20:26-28 NIV)

According to Jesus, believers qualify themselves for leadership when they are content to serve. Jesus is our example for this! A presence-based community is not a once-a-week gathering with the goal of being served. The new covenant community is a society of people who selflessly love one another according to the example of Jesus and the early Church. Instead of entitled consumers, members are both providers and recipients of the love of God. Each member of the community reveals the love of God to others as the presence of God enables and directs. Presence-based believers "love because he first loved us" (1 John 4:19 NIV)!

Chapter Six
INTIMACY

Intimacy with God is what humanity was created for. God's greatest desire is to live in and among His people. God *wants* to be known! He continually is cultivating our attention and affection. All humans are born with a longing for God, with a deep desire to be seen, known and loved by God. This longing exists in the heart and soul of all humanity as an internal "ache," a longing for "more." This longing for God is expressed in the full spectrum of human efforts to find meaning and significance in life. Many misunderstand this "hole in their soul" to be a desire for adventure; others attempt to fill this longing with riches or material wealth. Adventure and riches seem to provide a temporary solution. Some people attempt to cover the "hole" or fill its emptiness with food, drugs or alcohol. As time goes on, it becomes clear that none of these substitutions provides any lasting fulfillment. Instead, every seeker is left with a deeper desire for significance than before.

To continue their search for fulfillment, many seek significance in intimacy with others. Good friendships, meaningful conversation, group sports and even sexual intimacy produce significant meaning. But between encounters, a loneliness persists. In community with others, meaning and purpose grow more and more satisfying when participants love others with their heart, soul, mind and strength. Community is a medium of God's design for the expression and reception of His love on the earth. The love that can be expressed and received from friends and family creates community that is part of God's plan, but not the whole. But no person or group can bear the full weight of being loved by another with all of their heart, soul, mind and strength. Expectations shift, miscommunication happens and disappointments occur in even the most intimate of relationships. Eventually the love that was designed to be given to God is too weighty to be placed on any human foundation. The deepest fulfillment of our heart, soul, mind and body cannot be found among humans, but only in transparency and intimacy with God.

We discover that the longing within us to be fully known and loved was created by God. And God has that longing too, because we were created in His image.

Loving God with everything we are and have is not a wearisome burden but an amazing and satisfying journey. All of our being longs for this depth of relationship and meaning. Pouring out the fullness of our love and life to God is not like what we experience with other humans. God is a huge foundation, sufficient for the placement of all of our affections! He is the sacred source of all life and all creation! He is the source of love and purpose! He is without malice, pure and holy. He is mystical, creative, beautiful and full of wonder. Everything that He is, has been placed within our hearts to make us who we are. We long to know this true love in our heart of hearts because without Him our souls are starved for purpose and meaning. Our mind longs for knowledge and wisdom found only in Him, and even our bodies groan with all creation for the revelation of God!

Loving God with everything we are leads us right to a passionate, yielded relationship with the Spirit of God. Loving God with all of our heart means that we primarily pursue God as a lifestyle, seeking to encounter Him in worship and to "see His face" (rather than a gift from His hands) in prayer. Seeking His face means to seek God for *who He is* not for *what we want*! Loving God with all of the soul means that we live in creative pursuit of God, allowing

Him to guide our willfulness and creativity to reveal His glory on the earth. Loving God with all of our mind becomes an exciting, ongoing pursuit in the revelation of the knowledge of God and illumination of His creation. Finally, loving God with all of our strength requires perseverance and obedience in order to work and to speak for Him, revealing His Kingdom on the earth. In yielded intimacy with the Lord, we experience a pure heart, a transformed mind and a healthy body.

God's desire for intimacy with His people is revealed by Jesus in response to a question. When one of the teachers of the law asked Jesus which commandment was the greatest, Jesus answered, "Love the Lord your God with all your heart and with all your soul and with all your mind and with all your strength" (Mark 12:30 NIV). When Jesus affirmed this commandment, He was affirming the deepest desire of God for relationship with all people, starting with Adam. To be loved with the full force of passion (heart), with all the creative powers of the soul, with the deepest imaginations and thoughts of the mind, and with every fiber of the strength is not only the desire of God from His people, but also the desire of people for God. The desire to be fully loved is really in the heart of everyone. To know that an intimate relationship is a desire in the heart of God is very exciting, but to experience this relationship with God is not a one-way street.

The Offering
The Scriptures reveal that God's goal has always been to live in intimate relationship with His people. The design of all the covenants God made with Abraham, Moses and David was for the people of God to know Him by encounter in worship. Worship involves the presentation of one's self in a variety of ways to the Lord as an offering.

To encounter God in worship, during the period of the old covenant, God required His people to bring the best of their animals as a sacrifice or burnt offering. The goal of this encounter for God was to meet and speak with His people.

For the generations to come this burnt offering is to be made regularly at the entrance to the tent of meeting, before the

LORD. *There I will **meet you** and **speak to you**; there also **I will meet with the Israelites**, and the place will **be consecrated by my glory**.* (Exodus 29:42-43 NIV, emphasis added)

The people were called to gather in a place to worship that would be consecrated by God's glory! God's promise was that He would *consecrate* the place where they gathered with His glorious presence! The goal of worship has always been an encounter with God! The goal of meeting with God was intimacy—to meet with God and to hear God speak!

Worship is a presentation of one's self to God—to come before Him as an offering as well as to bring Him offerings so that He can meet with us. His response, according to the pattern we find in the Bible, is to consecrate this meeting with glory. God delights to reveal His fullness in response to the presentation of ourselves to Him. Worship is not the same as singing. Worship, rather, is measured in selfless adoration of God. The goal is not to appease His anger or to earn His love. The goal of worship is to minister *to* Him by the presentation of ourselves; our person to His Person. This is what is meant when the Bible commands us to "seek His face."

*Sing to him, sing praise to him; tell of all his wonderful acts. Glory in his holy name; **let the hearts of those who seek the LORD rejoice**. Look to the LORD and his strength; **seek his face always**.* (1 Chronicles 16:9-11 NIV, emphasis added)

Seeking the face of God does not involve asking Him for things. Seeking the face of God by presenting ourselves to Him is the primary method of ongoing encounter and intimacy with God. Consider the patterns of intimacy that we experience and enjoy with other people. When people enjoy being with one another and want to get to know one another better, they meet face to face. Some people call it "face time" or "hanging out." There is no agenda. Using biblical words, we can say that the goal for developing an intimate relationship with others is to "abide" or "remain" with them. A meeting "for lunch" or "for coffee" is not primarily about the lunch or the coffee! The lunch and the coffee is in essence "and offering" but the real goal is to present one's self. The goal in relationship is encounter: a face-to-face gathering for the purpose of getting to know one another more intimately. The relationship is not about the food being offered or the time being spent. It is about the depth of the encounter itself. It is about seeing their face, hearing their voice and getting to know what is in their heart and mind. That is intimacy!

Using the same pattern of encounter with other people, God has called us to encounter Him. God is "attracted to the table" by worship just like a friend is attracted to the table for "lunch," but the real offering is ourselves! We bring our offering of worship, but the goal of God is encounter and intimacy, not the offering.

A Kingdom of Priests
In the covenant of Moses, the people lived as God's servants. In the old covenant "serving" the Lord was the goal of the covenant rather than intimacy. The promises, stipulations, privileges and responsibilities in the covenant of Moses were more "transactional" in nature and were based primarily on commandments and observances that the people of God were required to obey. But this is not how God intended for it to be!

The original covenant of Moses started with an invitation for face-to-face worship and encounter. Three months after the people of Israel were miraculously delivered from Egypt, Moses brought *all* of them to the foot of Mount Sinai to worship God by meeting with Him at the foot of the mountain. God told Moses His plan for the people:

> "...Although the whole earth is mine, you will be for me **a kingdom of priests** and a holy nation." These are the words you are to speak to the Israelites. (Exodus 19:5-6 NIV, emphasis added)

God invited the people of Israel to meet with Him at the foot of the mountain. They were invited to be a *kingdom of priests*! For three days the people prepared to meet with God. They were told that on the third day, the Lord would come down on Mount Sinai in their sight and the Lord would give them the covenant. In the days leading up to this encounter, clouds began to gather on the mountain. The Bible tells us that the people began to become fearful at the prospect of this gathering. At the trumpet blast, they all gathered with Moses at the foot of the mountain to worship...

> *When the people saw the thunder and lightning and heard the trumpet and saw the mountain in smoke, they trembled with fear. They* **stayed at a distance** *and said to Moses,* **"Speak to us yourself and we will listen. But do not have God speak to us or we will die."** *Moses said to the people, "Do not be afraid. God has come to test you, so that the fear of God will be with you to keep you from sinning."* **The people remained at a distance,** *while Moses approached the thick darkness where God was.* (Exodus 20:18-21 NIV, emphasis added)

The people chose not participate in the opportunity to encounter God in worship! Why didn't they approach God and participate in God's amazing invitation? It seems that they entered into fear because they were afraid to die. The awesome presence and power of God was visible to them, but instead of approaching in yieldedness to worship, they refused! They chose instead to live according to the priesthood ministry of Moses. They chose to be *represented* before God by Moses. Because of their response, God did meet face to face with Moses, who the Bible tells us continually sought the face of the Lord (Deuteronomy 34:10).

Following the people's retreat from the presence of the Lord, God set apart the tribe of Levi as His priesthood. Instead of meeting with all the people face to face as He had with Moses, the Levites would serve the Lord on behalf of the people. They would also serve and minister to the people on behalf of the Lord. Instead of "consecrating" all the people to be set apart for God, the Lord called the Levites to be consecrated for all the Israelites. Conversely, instead of meeting with the people directly, God would minister to the people through the priesthood.

The primary role of the priesthood is "ministry" to the Lord. "Ministry to the Lord" means to be present to the Lord, to seek His face by waiting on Him and to exalt Him by worship in word, song and artistic expression. The rest of the people fulfilled their responsibilities of worship in four ways: obedience to His laws (including the sabbath), celebrating the religious feasts, participating in the sacrifices and attending the solemn assemblies led by the priests. Intimate relationship with God was reserved for prophets, priests and kings—those who led the people.

In the new covenant, worship is no longer the responsibility of an intermediary, a leader who serves as priest to worship for the people. Instead, the priesthood has been given to all who love God. In the old covenant, it was sufficient to attend the worship event. Confidence was placed in the priests to attend to the presence of the Lord while everyone else participated simply by gathering for the solemn assembly.

All members of the new covenant are called and enabled as a kingdom of priests to encounter God and minister to Him face to face! In yieldedness to God, all members of a presence-based community are given the access once only reserved for the temple priests. The Book of Revelation records a declaration describing the role of the presence-based priesthood in the new covenant. In this passage, elders and angels minister before the throne of God in heaven:

> *And they sang a new song, saying: "You are worthy to take the scroll and to open its seals, because you were slain, and with your blood you purchased for God persons from every tribe and language and people and nation. You have made them to be **a kingdom and priests to serve our God,** and they will reign on the earth."* (Revelation 5:9-10 NIV, emphasis added)

The invitation to be a kingdom of priests is the same one offered to God's people at the foot of Mount Sinai! Reigning as kings and serving Him as priests is the invitation of a presence-based community! Instead of being spectators, we are invited to be participants, to reign in partnership with Him on the earth!

The incredible challenge that faces the people of God in the new covenant are similar to the challenges that the people of God faced at Sinai! Will we worship God as He wants to be worshipped? Will the people of God be set apart and consecrated in preparation for worship

as they were called to be? Will we "enter in" to meet Him with yieldedness, knowing how worthy, holy and wonderful His is? Will we be as
selfless and desperate as Moses? Will we choose the ministry of worship over comfort and self-service? Instead of consumers who come
before God to receive from His hands, members of a presence-based
community approach God as the priesthood, in yieldedness to seek
His face and minister to him as a primary occupation.

Abiding

The way of intimacy was demonstrated by Jesus's lifestyle. He lived life
by "being one" with God. This enabled Him to reveal the glory (fullness) of God on the earth. Instead of cultivating intimacy with God
and then telling His disciples what He experienced, Jesus taught His
disciples how to be intimate with God by His relationship with them.
Jesus called this "abiding":

> **Abide in Me, and I in you.** As the branch cannot bear fruit
> of itself, unless it abides in the vine, neither can you, unless
> you abide in Me. I am the vine, you are the branches. **He who
> abides in Me, and I in him, bears much fruit**; for without Me
> you can do nothing. If anyone does not abide in Me, he is cast
> out as a branch and is withered; and they gather them and
> throw them into the fire, and they are burned. If you abide in
> Me, and My words abide in you, you will ask what you desire,
> and it shall be done for you. By this My Father is glorified, that
> you bear much fruit; so you will be My disciples. (John 15:4-11
> NIV, emphasis added)

Western Christianity tends to interpret the phrase "abiding in
Christ" as meaning the same as "being saved." But this passage is not
about salvation; it is about "producing fruit." Jesus emphasized bearing
fruit in much of His teaching. He used the word *fruit* thirty-four times
in the four Gospels.

Fruit is never a reference to salvation. Instead, fruitfulness is used
to describe attitudes and actions that are produced as a result of being in relationship with God. Instead of "being saved," this passage

is about the attitudes and actions that are "produced" in our lives by intimacy and participation with Jesus.

According to this teaching, branches that abide (those that are attached to the vine by maintaining vital connection) will produce much fruit. Those who are attached but do not "abide" wither and die. In John 15, Jesus is describing what happens when believers become attached to Him and are *yielded to receive* all that He has for them. This process of abiding produces fruit (attitudes and actions) that come from Jesus.

According to this passage, the only way to be fruitful is to be intimately connected with Jesus. Then the fruit (the actions and attitudes) that this intimacy produces will become evident! So, what is the fruit that we produce? What actions and attitudes are produced when we are intimately connected to Jesus? Paul gave a list these attitudes and actions that he called the fruit of the Spirit:

> *But the fruit of the Spirit is love, joy, peace, longsuffering, kindness, goodness, faithfulness, gentleness, self-control. Against such there is no law. And those who are Christ's have crucified the flesh with its passions and desires. If we live in the Spirit, let us also walk in the Spirit.* (Galatians 5:22-25 NKJV)

The means of producing this fruit of the Spirit, Paul explained, is to "walk by the Spirit" (Galatians 5:16 NIV). He also described this as "keeping in step" with the Spirit (Galatians 5:25 NIV). Yieldedness to the Spirit of God is the means of allowing Him to produce the character of God in our lives according to this passage.

In the new covenant, the work of God to transform us into His image is not achieved by work or knowledge; instead, it is achieved by abiding. God is love. In His presence is fullness of joy. He is peaceful and patient, kind and good to all. He is faithful, gentle and self-controlled. (See 1 John 4:8; Psalm 16:11 and Exodus 34-5-7.) And so we will become loving, joyful, peaceful, patient, kind, good, faithful, gentle and self-controlled as we abide in Him.

The fruit of the Spirit is the character of God that *He* produces in us as *we* maintain our vital connection to the presence of God. The vine does not work to produce fruit. The fruit proliferates as a natural result of abiding. This doesn't mean that it is easy! In fact, learning to die to self and remain connected to the life-transforming work of God is a lifelong journey of incredible surrender and amazing fruitfulness! Fruitfulness also means that God "prunes" the branches so that they will bear more fruit (John 15:2). God is very interested in fruitfulness, even at the expense of our comfort! Our responsibility is abiding—out of which all the works of righteousness are produced. A transformation happens as we abide in Christ. Paul told us:

> *Therefore, if anyone is in Christ, he is a new creation; old things have passed away; behold, all things have become new.* (2 Corinthians 5:17 NKJV)

This very well-known verse has often been quoted with the understanding that being "in Christ" means salvation. But this verse isn't about salvation; it's about being a new creation. We are all aware that most individuals don't suddenly become "a new person" when they get saved. In fact, the change that can be seen *starts* with salvation, but a new creation is what being "in Christ" produces. The phrase "in Christ" is used eighty-five times in the New Testament and never refers to salvation but rather shows attachment (such as "faith in Christ" or "life in Christ") by abiding in Christ. Being "in Christ" is not a transaction but a relationship with Him.

The Coming Reformation

Is "abiding in Him" one of the primary goals of the Church in North America? If abiding in Christ produces transformation of character (attitude and action) in those who participate, then we should be able to see a radical difference in lifestyle between the Church and the world.

George Barna began polling Christians in the United States in 1984. Every year the Barna Group collects data about the Church and U.S. culture at large. In 2014, the Barna Group released the results of its poll regarding the attitudes and the behaviors of both "born-again" believers and non-churchgoers. They compared the attitudes and behaviors of both of these groups and discovered that there was virtually no difference in any measurable sense between the Church and the world.[1] Born-again believers report the same levels of unhappiness, depression and anger and experience divorce and broken relationships at the same rate as the world!

Can we blame this lack of spiritual fruit on poor knowledge of the Bible? Can we point to a lack of desire that believers in the U.S. have to know God? Maybe the reason for the results is related to laziness on behalf of those who go to church. Of course, the answer is "no" to each of these propositions. Nearly all believers know what God requires of them. All who know about Jesus want His attitudes and character in themselves. Being lazy or inactive is probably not the problem either. In fact, one of many criticisms of the American Church is that most local churches are operated like a business rather than community of faith.[2] Would it help to develop a fruit-producing curriculum or related church program? Of course not. There is no lack of programs, information and activity in the Western Church. Instead of doing more, we need to do less. Instead of working harder to be fruitful, God calls the Western Church to "seek His face" and live in intimacy with Him in order to be fruitful.

A second reformation of the Western Church is needed—a reformation of the same magnitude as the first. The present dark age of materialism, consumerism and entitlement has created so many barriers to yieldedness. It seems as though the meaning of these Scriptures is almost beyond the comprehension of the Western Church. A radical change is needed. A new start—a "reboot"—in the character and function of the Western Church is needed.

As I write this, the world is truly suffering in the grips of the worldwide COVID-19 pandemic. In response to the threat of sickness and possible death, many churches have closed their doors. What will happen during this season? Will the remnant Church of Jesus Christ take this opportunity to step out from the ranks of churchgoers to truly worship and seek the face of God? Will they become disciplined in order to live in yieldedness to reveal His power and purposes on the earth?

Jesus promised that the indwelling Spirit would "guide [us] into all the truth" (John 16:13 NIV). This means that as we give our attention to the Spirit of God, we will learn through abiding in Him what we should do and where we should go. Instead of teaching people what to do next by learning about the Bible, we pray together and seek the Lord for His guidance in our lives. In accordance with His Word, the Spirit within us reveals the deep things of God.

> *But as it is written: "Eye has not seen, nor ear heard, nor have entered into the heart of man the things which God has prepared for those who love Him."* **But God has revealed them to us through His Spirit. For the Spirit searches all things, yes, the deep things of God.** *For what man knows the things of a man except the spirit of the man which is in him? Even so* **no one knows the things of God except the Spirit of God.** *Now we have received, not the spirit of the world, but the Spirit who is from God, that we might know the things that have been freely given to us by God. These things we also speak,* **not in words which man's wisdom teaches but which the Holy Spirit teaches,** *comparing spiritual things with spiritual.* (1 Corinthians 2:9-13 NKJV, emphasis added)

A presence-based community is a community of people who live in communion with God. By waiting on the Lord, the Spirit of God reveals the "deep things" of God. The passage teaches us that the wisdom that we receive from God is spiritual rather than worldly. Rather than doing what we want or what seems right from a worldly perspective, the Spirit of God reveals His spiritual wisdom. Instead of thinking about what to do and doing what is right in our own eyes, the Spirit is the Counselor leading the community in what to do and where to go.

Making disciples was the commission of Jesus. How did Jesus make disciples and what did He teach them? He taught them to pray. He taught His disciples to heal the sick, raise the dead and cast out demons. He showed them how to live in love toward one another and how to care and serve others. Just before He laid down His life, He commanded them to wait on God. With prayer and supplication, the disciples practiced the discipline of seeking God's face—waiting and watching. By encounter, the Spirit of God came upon them to give them purpose and power. This presence-based community experienced guidance about where to go and what to do by means of the presence of God within them. This is the nature of the coming reformation of the Church.

God has not called us to go to church; God has called us to *be* the Church. In these days of testing, God is removing every last vestige of transactional religion. He is refining the goals of our meetings. He is refining us to remove the dross of "spectator Christianity." The enemy of our soul will do anything to keep us from abiding. Instead of being plugged in to the source of life and power, believers are attempting to live, essentially, without abiding, so they struggle to obtain the fruit of the Spirit (love, joy, peace, patience, kindness, goodness, faithfulness, gentleness and self-control) within them. How can we produce love and power if we are not "plugged in" (abiding in) the Source of love and power? Intimacy with God provides the power for fruitfulness, guidance and purpose in the presence-based community!

Chapter Seven
THE PRIESTHOOD

The presence-based community that was established by Jesus and described in the Bible is a *kingdom of priests* (Revelation 5:10). Instead of Christians who gather for a weekly meeting, a presence-based community is a community of priests living out of relationship with God and in relationship with one another to reveal God's glory and extend His kingdom on the earth. Rather than ruling by entitlement or reward, this kingdom of priests is purchased by the blood of Jesus and they are set apart for Him. Beyond the imagination of any one person, the Kingdom of God is the revelation of God's love and His amazing original purposes on the earth. It is the atmosphere of Heaven. It is what Jesus taught His disciples to pray for!

> *So He said to them, "When you pray, say: Our Father in heaven, hallowed be Your name. **Your kingdom come. Your will be done on earth as it is in heaven.**" (Luke 11:2 NKJV, emphasis added)*

The purpose of the priesthood is to live in consecration and partnership with God for the revelation of His Kingdom on the earth, just as it is in heaven.

Rather than performing daily or weekly acts of worship in a central location like the priests of the old covenant, the priesthood of the new covenant follows the lifestyle of Jesus. Jesus was not a solitary being. In fact, Jesus's lifestyle was one that regularly cultivated and maintained relationship with others. Jesus lived and taught that intentional relationships with others were at the *center* of what it means to be a presence-based community!

The example of Jesus is always our model. Jesus lived in unbroken partnership with God. His life so perfectly demonstrated oneness with God that He told His disciples, "He who has seen Me, has seen the Father" (John 14:9 NKJV). This oneness was not accomplished by living in the wilderness; nor was it achieved by going about life without attention to prayer. Jesus practiced a balanced lifestyle. It is what we will call "spiritual breathing."

Spiritual Breathing
Spiritual breathing is a balance between a life of *being* with God and *doing* for God. Jesus gave His *primary* attention to periods of personal encounter with God. Just like breathing, there is no vitality without first "breathing in" the life-giving atmosphere. Jesus gave His attention to connecting with God in regular periods described in the Bible. For instance, the Bible tells us that Jesus "often withdrew to lonely places and prayed" (Luke 5:16 NIV). This "breathing in" perpetuated the vibrant life of God within Jesus. By partnering with God, this *being* with God resulted in *doing* mighty miracles. It was not the divinity of Jesus Himself that enabled Him to speak with authority and minister with power: it was the presence of God ministering through Jesus by the proclamation of the gospel.

Jesus ministry was accomplished by "breathing out" the same atmosphere of the presence of God within Him. Instead of a separation of the sacred and secular, the example and lifestyle of Jesus reveals that—for Jesus—there was no separation. Jesus carried the Kingdom of God with Him because the Kingdom of God is whenever and wherever God reigns. Jesus did not treat "sinners" differently. In fact,

He was often criticized by the religious leaders for associating with them (Luke 5:20; 15:2). This was offensive to the Pharisees because they taught that those who were sacred did not associate with those who were secular.

Jesus revealed that the Kingdom is *not* in one place or another. Jesus told them, "The kingdom of God is within you" (Luke 17:21 NKJV). The lifestyle of Jesus and the first presence-based community consisted of a rhythm, a balance of life. They lived with intentionality by breathing in by communion with God first and then breathing out this life of God in mutual ministry and communion with others. Ministry to the Lord empowers ministry to others. Without a connection to the life-giving Spirit of God very little life can be shared. The love of God in those who seek His face enables them by love to serve others while being involved in the regular activities of daily life.

Holiness to the Lord

The primary calling of priests is to be set apart to the Lord. God is not primarily interested in the work that we can do for Him; rather, God is very interested in us. He is not looking for employees; He is looking for lovers. The primary work of the priesthood is to be set apart to God.

This condition of being set apart for God is called holiness. Holiness is necessary. "Without holiness no one will see the Lord," declared the writer of Hebrews (Hebrews 12:14 NIV). Holiness is a requirement for intimacy with the presence of God. As a priesthood, a presence-based community is consecrated *to* God and *for* God as a primary calling by cultivating holiness.

In accordance with the greatest commandment, loving God with our heart, soul, mind and strength is our primary calling. This requires that we be set apart. Holiness is necessary because sin causes separation from the life of God. Isaiah declared:

> *Surely the arm of the LORD is not too short to save, nor his ear too dull to hear. But your iniquities have separated you from your God; your sins have hidden his face from you, so that he will not hear.* (Isaiah 59:1-2 NIV)

A separation occurs between God and His people when they purposely turn away from participation with Him. This separation is not due to a disability on God's part! (His arm is not too short!) Instead, this passage indicates that it is our *iniquities* that have *separated* us; our *sins* have *hidden* His face so that He cannot hear. In this passage, these two words *iniquities* and *sins* point to specific behaviors. The original Hebrew word translated as "sin" means "missing the mark"[1] and the word for "iniquity" means to "twist or distort."[2] Iniquity can be understood to mean purposeful wrongdoing while sin seems to indicate any misdeed that "misses the mark."

Holiness in the new covenant occurs by being set apart in our affections for God. In the new covenant, God is raising up a holy nation that is set apart for Him. A presence-based community does not live in the old covenant "sin and repent" cycle. Instead, a presence-based community lives in relationship with Jesus as a *royal priesthood*:

> But **you are a chosen people, a royal priesthood, a holy nation**, *God's special possession, that you may declare the praises of him who called you out of darkness into his wonderful light. Once you were not a people, but now you are the people of God; once you had not received mercy, but now you have received mercy. Dear friends, I urge you,* **as foreigners and exiles, to abstain from sinful desires, which wage war against your soul.** *Live such good lives among the pagans that, though they accuse you of doing wrong, they may see your good deeds and glorify God on the day he visits us.* (1 Peter 2:9-12 NIV, emphasis added)

As a royal priesthood, who are set apart for God, intimacy with the presence of God is threatened and even broken by sin. As we grow in true love, sin becomes distasteful and even foreign to us. Instead of feeling at home in the kingdom of this world, a royal priesthood (a kingdom of priests) gains a passion for the presence of God that invalidates a passion for darkness and falsehood. A true love for God necessitates *and* empowers believers to refrain from all that does not please Him. By loving God with all of our heart, soul, mind and strength, our affections are reset. Instead of working *for* the love of God, we work *out* of the love that is in us.

Love motivates a lifestyle of holiness rather than the fear of judgment, which is the motivation for the "sin and repent" pattern of the old covenant. Instead of fearing judgment, we enjoy the transforming work of God. By keeping in step with the leading of the Spirit of God, we discover that the desire for sin decreases.

> *So I say,* **walk by the Spirit, and you will not gratify the desires of the flesh**. *For the flesh desires what is contrary to the Spirit, and the Spirit what is contrary to the flesh. They are in conflict with each other, so that you are not to do whatever you want. But if you are led by the Spirit, you are not under the law.* (Galatians 5:16-18 NIV, emphasis added)

Paul explained that keeping in step with the Spirit of God has an inverse relationship to fulfilling the desires of the flesh! The original language is clear. Paul was actually saying that the more you walk in the Spirit, the less you will gratify your sinful nature. Then he made a startling statement in verse 18: "If you are led by the Spirit, then you are not under the law"! Does this mean that we no longer have to obey the Ten Commandments? Absolutely not! Does this mean that the people in a presence-based community do whatever they feel is right? Not at all!

The truth is that a true presence-based community exhibits a level of holiness that far exceeds any in the old covenant. Instead of daily struggling with sin, a presence-based community experiences the guidance and empowerment of the Spirit of God within giving us the power and the purpose to live like Jesus did. By living in yieldedness to the Spirit, we become aware of what God wants. By following the Spirit of God, we have the power to resist sin. In fellowship with the Spirit, we can avoid any iniquity. If we continue to live under the old covenant, we do not have the guidance of the Spirit to know what sin is or have the power to overcome it.

In fact, the writers of the New Testament reveal to us in several passages that we must avoid living "under the law" and live instead "under grace" (Romans 6:14; Galatians 5:4). By living "under grace," we do not engage in the old covenant "sin and repent" pattern because the precepts of God are written on our hearts and the power of the Spirit is within us to overcome the dominion of darkness. Just as Jeremiah prophesied, the Spirit of God "writes His precepts on our hearts" so that we know the will of God (Jeremiah 31:33). Under "grace" we have been given the "authority to overcome all the power of the enemy" (Luke 10:19 NIV)!

Worship
The priests in the old covenant were commissioned in divisions to minister in the Holy Place before the Lord for twelve-hour shifts during an entire week from sabbath to sabbath. The priests would wash from head to toe and be anointed before putting on a clean and spotless white robe. Only then did they enter to worship. During their week of ministry to the Lord in the Holy Place, the priests would worship the Lord by playing harps and singing in worship before the Lord. They were also commissioned to "seek His face" (1 Chronicles 16:11 NKJV) and to pray on behalf of the people while keeping the incense on the altar burning day and night (Exodus 30:8).

The Bible tells us that during this time the manifest presence of the Lord remained in the Holy of Holies just behind the heavy, many-layered veil (Exodus 30:6). Day and night, worship and prayer took place just outside the Holy of Holies. Only once a year did the high priest enter this hallowed place with the blood of the yearly sacrifice to offer atonement for all the people of Israel and to minister in the presence of the Lord.However, when Jesus fulfilled the requirements of the old covenant on the cross, the veil of the temple was torn. Now the presence of the Lord was made accessible for all of those who would worship Him "in the beauty of holiness" (1 Chronicles 16:29 NKJV).

Humans are created for worship. However, authentic worship seems mysterious to Western minds. Once again, this is due to our unfamiliarity with sovereignty. The image of one person "bowing down" to sovereign Lord or King in honor seems extremely out of place in contemporary culture. Westerners can imagine worship occurring in other places—of people bowing down with their faces to the floor in obeisance to an idol in a temple, for instance—but we feel as though this is a practice for "less advanced" people. Nothing could be further from the truth.

The *Oxford Dictionary* defines worship as "the feeling or expression of reverence and adoration."[3] Worship is not dead in Western society; in fact, it is practiced in regular intervals by all. Instead of the feeling or expression of reverence and adoration for one image, the people in Western culture venerate millions. These images are produced for us at a rate of multiples-a-minute through our televisions, computers and smart phones. Instead of spending one hour a day in feelings of adoration for one object (as we imagine worship to be), we spend many hours with intense attention and devotion to images in the thousands. One could argue that it is not worship that western people are participating in when they are watching television or their computer screen. One might say that this participation is just entertainment or meaningful communication.

I would like to make a proposal. I propose that if someone were to spend an average of three hours or more *each day* looking with adoration and intense interest at any one thing or person that this behavior might indicate idolatry. If you believe what I propose, then you will be shocked to know that most Americans are truly practicing idolatry!

A Nielson Company Report from 2016 shows that Americans spend an average of ten *hours and thirty-nine minutes in front of a screen each day!*[4] That's t*en hours a day* as an average! This means that some people are sitting adoringly for *more* than ten hours each day!

Within each person is the yearning for beauty. We have an innate desire to seek and adore objects of superlative power, purpose and creativity. The giving of our attention, time and resources is the purest measure of worship. Given this definition, everyone worships something. Self-worship is the spirit of the age. Giving your time, resources and attention to serve yourself does not mean that you don't have an object of worship; it simply means that the object of your worship is you!

God is the only One worthy of our worship. He is worthy of all our time, attention and resources because He created all good things. Our due service is to give Him thanks for all that He does. Just because of who He is, He is worthy of all praise.

He loves to be thanked. He loves to be praised. Why would God desire our thanks? Why would God want humans to adore Him and remind Him of His wonder and power by declaring His mighty works (Psalm 145:4)? How do we know this? Because He has asked us to offer our thanksgiving as we gather and to offer our praise when we meet with Him (Psalm 100:4). As much as it seems strange that an omniscient God would want to hear us tell Him things that He already knows about Himself, this is truly what He wants. Perhaps it is not difficult to understand after all; every human is created in His image, and everyone, without exception, loves to be thanked for what they do and be noticed for who they are. In this way, we truly are made in the likeness of God!

God is worthy! He is worthy of all thanksgiving, worship and praise. This is the true reason for worship. All of creation inspires our worship for Him! He is worthy to be praised for His presence in our lives, for ample food, water, shelter, warmth—the list goes on! God surrounds Himself with worship in the heavenlies:

> *Then I looked and heard the voice of many angels, number-ing thousands upon thousands, and ten thousand times ten thousand. They encircled the throne and the living creatures and the elders. In a loud voice they were saying: "Worthy is the Lamb, who was slain, to receive power and wealth and wisdom and strength and honor and glory and praise!" Then I heard every creature in heaven and on earth and under the earth and on the sea, and all that is in them, saying: "To him who sits on the throne and to the Lamb be praise and honor and glory and power, for ever and ever!" The four living crea-tures said, "Amen," and the elders fell down and worshiped.* (Revelation 5:11-14 NIV)

As the priesthood, it is our privilege to minister to God in wor-ship. We bow before Him in prayer. We are honored to gather for seasons in His presence to worship. A presence-based community gathers not just to sing songs but to give attention to an encounter with God. We come before Him to worship Him in Spirit and truth. Jesus defines the nature of worship in the new covenant:

> *Yet a time is coming and has now come when **the true worshipers will worship the Father in the Spirit and in truth,** for they are the kind of worshipers the Father seeks. God is spirit, and his worshipers must worship in the Spirit and in truth.* (John 4:23-24 NIV, emphasis added)

The time is now come! The people of God are the priesthood! God is looking for worshippers who will worship in spirit and truth! The presence of God is present to those who worship. The promise of God is to be with us when we gather to worship: "For where two or three gather in my name, there am I with them" (Matthew 18:20 NIV).

Worship is the mechanism of attracting the presence of God. God is looking for worshippers and has promised to gather with us as we gather in His name. God has promised to draw near to His people when they draw near to Him (James 4:8) In worship, we gather with unveiled faces to encounter His glory:

> *Now the Lord is the Spirit, and where the Spirit of the Lord is, there is freedom. And we all, who with unveiled faces contemplate the Lord's glory, are being transformed into his image with ever-increasing glory, which comes from the Lord, who is the Spirit.* (2 Corinthians 3:17-18 NIV)

In the presence of God, worshipping believers are transformed into the image of Jesus! Believers bring themselves as an offering and God transforms us with His ever-increasing glory into who we were created to be!

Authentic worship is our priesthood ministry to the Lord. This priesthood ministry is not like attending a funeral. The priesthood ministry is more like attending a music festival! Clapping, shouting, bowing down and lying prostrate on the floor are all biblical forms of worship and can be done as expressions of the priesthood worship in private and public gatherings. It is important to allow all participants to respond to the Lord in obedience. It is also important that these expressions not distract from allowing others to worship. The discipline of yieldedness must guide the practice of corporate worship. Paul described this balance:

> *You, my brothers and sisters, were called to be free. But do not use your freedom to indulge the flesh; rather, serve one another humbly in love.* (Galatians 5:13 NIV)

Seasons of worship, of gathering to worship in song and to wait on the Lord (as the main event), is one of the primary ways that a presence-based community gathers for the priesthood ministry. When the Church gathers in "one accord," the presence of God is *given room* to move and minister to the saints (Acts 2:1). Singing songs is quite different than worshipping with them. Playing skillfully is important, but skill of execution is not a measure of authentic worship.

Authentic corporate and personal expressions of worship take place in four ways: celebration, thanksgiving, praise and adoration.

Celebration is the authentic and joyful expression of our hearts to God. God loves it when we celebrate! Celebration is not optional! All living traditions have celebrations! This is what gives life to a gathering! Celebration consists of songs that declare the wonder of God. Celebration is culturally variable. Some cultures celebrate by gathering quietly to light candles and sing. Other cultures sponsor several days of feasting, dancing and worshipping and singing! The old covenant was full of feast days, feasts and assemblies with singing and dancing in celebration to the Lord. These celebrations often lasted for weeks.

Thanksgiving is offered to God for what He has done for us. We must thank God when we gather in His name! The actions of God are the focus for thanksgiving. Thanksgiving can be expressed in words, song, dance or even artistic expression. We are commanded to give thanks to the Lord (Psalm 106:1). He is worthy! We most often express our thanksgiving by praying prayers or singing songs of thanksgiving to God. The Bible also teaches us that the consequences of not being thankful are catastrophic. Those who are not thankful suffer with futile thinking and darkened hearts (Romans 1:21 NIV). Could thanklessness alone account for the condition of our current society?

Praise is given to God because of who He is. He is worthy, so when a presence-based community gathers praise to God is a first order of business! A presence-based community lives for opportunities to praise God. The focus of praise is on the character of God. Praise affirms who God is and identifies His wonderful traits. Singing, speaking, dancing or even creating artistic expressions (for example, painting or sculpting) can be authentic expressions of affirming the nature of God in praise. One of the most powerful ways to express praise for God's character is in the form of artistic expression. Painting, sculpting or crafting works of art can carry a subtle yet powerful expression in praise. Such artwork can carry deep meanings and expanded understandings of the nature of God that are beyond words. In praise, God is magnified.

Adoration is the passionate expression of our hearts in worship to God. When the people of God gather to Adore Jesus, Jesus Himself is present among us because He loves to be adored! Adoration is drawing near to God in single-minded devotion:

> *Come near to God and he will come near to you. Wash your hands, you sinners, and purify your hearts, you double-minded.* (James 4:8 NIV)

The response of God to adoration is amazing. The presence of God is drawn to hearts who are expressing worship with authentic devotion. Adoration is very intimate. It often takes the form of kneeling, lying on the floor during corporate times of worship, and waiting on the Lord. There are many ways that people have given adoration to the Lord in the Scriptures. Some of the most powerful expressions of adoration can be done by dancing and artistic expression. Adoration is accomplished by heart-to-heart communion with God.

In all these ways, the kingdom of priests that Jesus purchased with his blood ministers to the Lord as a primary occupation. But worship is not measured by sound or time, worship is truly measured by the authenticity of its expression. This is something that only God sees. God will reveal His love and power to all who truly worship Him in Spirit and truth; after all, these "are the kind of worshipers the Father seeks" (John 4:23 NIV).

Chapter Eight

MANIFESTATION

The Spirit of God longs to be revealed on the earth. At Pentecost, the presence of God that had been manifest in Jesus's life and ministry became manifest in those whom He had set apart for Himself. A spiritual manifestation is an *observable* event (or pattern of events) that clearly reveals the existence and power of an *unobservable* presence or power. A common form of speech that accurately captures the meaning of this word is "to show up."

The presence of God loves to show up among His people! God wants to reveal Himself to all those who earnestly seek Him.

> *For I know the thoughts that I think toward you, says the LORD, thoughts of peace and not of evil, to give you a future and a hope. Then you will **call upon Me** and **go and pray to Me**, and I will listen to you. **And you will seek Me and find Me, when you search for Me with all your heart.*** (Jeremiah 29:11-13 NKJV, emphasis added)

The pattern for an encounter with God has always been the same: when the people of God seek Him humbly and earnestly He makes

Himself known. Those who are seeking to know God will pursue Him according to His agenda—by worshipping and waiting. This type of seeking "creates room" for the presence of God to be revealed. The Church of Jesus Christ is designed to be a manifestation (a showcase) of the presence of Jesus to the world. For this reason, Paul called the Church, "the body of Christ" (1 Corinthians 12:27). Paul specifically used this term "body of Christ" to describe the presence-based function of the Church in the world.

The word for "church" in the original language means "called out ones" or those who have been set apart for God.[1] The word *church* is never used to refer to a building in the Bible. The Church is comprised of the people of God "called out" from the world; they are commissioned to minister in His name. Following Jesus is not a solitary religion. There is no example in history, starting with Jesus and the twelve disciples, of solitary Christianity. It is entirely against the plan of God for individual believers to live in isolation without regular and non-optional contact with other believers. A presence-based community will always meet face-to-face no matter what oppositions or prohibitions are placed against it. This is the nature and testimony of the church in history. The church has survived and thrived under; Roman persecution, the Inquisition, the Black Death, atheism, secularism and all manner of resistance. No matter what resistance it has faced, the church of Jesus will always gather in His name.

Many "born-again" believers at this time in history have chosen not to gather with others due to the restrictions or preference. This reveals the true condition of the church in the early 21st century. In this season, God is doing away with spectator Christianity. This refining period will bring the church into the full fruition of its purpose and power. God is calling and empowering the priesthood of believers to gather -at all costs- to minister in encounter with God and minister in love to one to another.

Jesus's last meeting with His followers has been called "The Great Commission." This commission of the first presence-based community is important. Jesus revealed through this commission the ways that He wants to be revealed to the world. This commission is for us as well. The same thing that the disciples were commissioned to do is what a presence-based community of today has been "called out" and commissioned to do.

Jesus's commission can be found in two places. In Mark 16:14-20, Jesus commissioned His followers to proclaim the good news. He told them that signs will accompany their ministry and that they will have authority to drive out demons and speak in new tongues. Jesus also told them that they will be protected against harm and that they will heal the sick. These are the signs and wonders that God revealed through Jesus's ministry. Since Jesus is "the author and the finisher of our faith" (Hebrews 12:2 NKJV), then the revelation of healing signs and wonders is actually the manifestation of Jesus's presence and ministry to the world. Matthew's Gospel records that Jesus also commissioned them to "make disciples."

Making disciples does not mean "make converts." When Jesus commanded his followers to "make disciples" He was actually commanding them to use the process that He demonstrated. Specifically, Jesus made disciples by inviting them to walk alongside of him. He baptized them and then taught them to obey God. He taught them how to pray and live in yieldedness to God and how to minister to others in the power of Spirit. Finally, Jesus promised that His presence would be with them always (Matthew 28:18-20)! This is exactly the pattern of Jesus life and ministry including the promise to be with them! Jesus lived in constant fellowship with the Father, in the same way Jesus promised to remain in constant fellowship with each disciple in their life and ministry. Jesus was called out by God to reveal God's love and power to the world. In turn, Jesus was commissioning His "called out" ones to continue to reveal God's love and power on the earth as He had been doing!

Before believers learn to live in yielded partnership with the Lord, the presence of God seems to be hidden from view. After learning to seek God according to His will, a manifestation of His presence occurs. God will only be revealed when He is provided room to move. The manifestation of God occurs in many ways, but most believers have trouble "seeing" God, recognizing the presence of God and then being confident enough to give him room to move. This process of seeing, recognizing and giving God room to move must be learned!

Seeing God

Very often the Spirit of God will show up in small ways. For believers who have not "made room" by cultivating the discipline of waiting or watching for the presence of God, these "movements" of the Spirit can go by undetected.

I love to be outdoors. Every fall I enjoy hiking. I have spent hours sitting silently in the woods just enjoying creation. I have seen squirrels, rabbits, grouse, foxes, racoons and bigger animals such as bobcats, deer and even bear. My wife and I live on a wooded, one-and-a-half-acre plot in the country. Because we live in a wooded area, we often see deer in the woods close to our home. One day, a good friend of mine, came by for a visit. We were both standing by the large picture window that overlooks our wooded backyard. Both of us were looking out the window as we talked. When I walked closer to the window, I immediately noticed a doe and two fawns grazing in the woods. I was watching them as my friend and I talked, but I noticed that he did not see them. At a break in the conversation, I commented, "Hey, look at the deer." My friend turned to look but he did respond. Instead, he remained looking out the window with a puzzled look on his face. I was surprised when he told me that he could not see anything! It was truly amazing because all three of the deer were so visible to me! Two of them were standing in the open just fifty feet away! As we were both standing there in front of the window, I began pointing out where they were. Just as I was beginning to describe what I was seeing, one of the deer moved. At that moment, he exclaimed, "Oh! I see it!" Within a few seconds he said, "There's a second one!" A minute later, he reported that he was able to see all three. It was amazing to me that he wasn't able to see them until I pointed them out AND they started to move.

I thought about the situation later. Even though it was just a matter of seeing deer in my back yard, it seemed that this situation contained some interesting parallels about the ways that God is present but remains undetected in the lives of His people.

I thought about the situation. Why was I able to see the deer, but my friend was not? Even when I called them his attention to them he was still not able to see them! Perhaps it was because I was used to seeing them in my backyard and knew that they might "show up" there.

I wondered if maybe he couldn't see them because he had no expectation of seeing anything. He wasn't thinking about animals. Although they were standing there the whole time he was unaware of their existence until I called His attention to them. Things changed only slightly when I told him that they were there. Even though he did not see them right away, just looking for "something" created an expectation in him. He was able to see one and then shortly all three after I pointed them out, but not while they were simply standing there. It was only when he "made room" in his mind to see the deer and was looking for them that they "showed up" because he could see them move. Suddenly it made sense to my why people who are not looking or expectant to "see" God struggle with making room for encounter with Him!

Recognizing God
God is always with us but often we don't see him or feel His presence with us.

I recall several events in my life in which I encountered situations beyond my control. In these situations, I lose track of the presence of God and begin to feel confused or anxious. Like a storm brewing in my mind, my feelings seem to "cloud over." In response to this anxiety, I attempt to calm myself, but sometimes it only gets worse. I know that God is with me, but somehow I can't see Him past the problem. I know He is there, but I don't "see" Him or feel His presence with me.

Then I say a quiet prayer, "God, help me!" At that moment, I begin to move in my thoughts away from the darkness and I fix the "eyes of my heart" on Jesus. It's not easy. It takes time. Sometimes I don't easily "see" Him because of the darkness that seems to be around me. It's as if I am "looking" for some "movement" in the darkness. I start to "make room" in my heart by giving Him my time and attention. It's as if I am holding my heart open for His touch. This expectation to see, even when I don't see right away, is very important. Then, somehow, usually within minutes (sometimes hours), I begin to sense that something is happening. The presence of God will quietly begin to "show up"—almost like the sun peering through the clouds a little at first. After a while, I am fully aware that He is with me and that all is well, no matter what is going on around me. Although God was there all along, it took me a while to "make room" for Him to be revealed in my heart and mind. In addition, it took some time for me to fix "the eyes of my heart" on God in faith (believing in what I had not yet seen) to experience God's presence in my life. Paul talked about this capacity that we have for "seeing God":

> *I pray that the **eyes of your heart** may be enlightened in order that you may **know the hope to which he has called you**, the riches of his glorious inheritance in his holy people.* (Ephesians 1:18 NIV, emphasis added)

God has given us spiritual senses with eyes to see what He is doing in our lives but we may struggle at times with the ability to see Him. Paul was praying for the Ephesians that they would be enlightened with the hope of God's calling. The eyes of the heart are the way that we see and experience God. Rather than seeing something visible to the human eye, the eyes of the heart are able to detect the activity of the Spirit of God.

The Spirit of God is *with* all who belong to Him. Jesus promised in John 14:16 that the Counselor will never leave us. However, we don't always see or feel Him. Our desire is for the presence of God to "show up" but at times the circumstances around us seem to create a situation where "seeing" Him or even "making room" for Him is difficult. In addition, it can be extremely difficult to take our focus off of the events and people around us to allow us to "see" Him and to experience His move among us. We may not see him because we are distracted or perhaps we don't expect to see Him. Similar to the situation with my friend, we must become aware that God is with us. Once we are aware that He is among us we can learn to "fix the eyes of our hearts" on Him, then we can and will experience His move in our lives.

Sin can affect this situation. Sin is a barrier to seeing God. Purposeful sin can make it impossible to see or feel God moving in our lives. It's not God's anger that separates us from Him; it is our departure from connection with Him. When we sin, we have chosen to go our way without Him. The only way to rejoin Him is by repentance and obedience.

Often the Spirit of God will show up in small ways when we gather in His name. All of us have experienced such manifestations. During a Sunday service or small group meeting, maybe during a time of prayer, a season of worship or during the message, it seems as though God "shows up" in unexpected ways to bring a sense of His comfort, conviction or peace. At other times, it seems that certain words are spoken that resonate in the hearts of some or all who are gathered, producing conviction and providing an opportunity for repentance and transformation. These are wonderful moments in the life of the Church. We all long for these moments when God moves in these unexpected ways. These experiences confirm that God's love for us is real and that He is among us.

Encounter and transformation by the presence of God is why the Church gathers. More often than not, these encounters with God occur within the context of friendships and the mutual care that takes place. In fact, the Kingdom of God is revealed as Jesus said, "The kingdom of God is in your midst" (Luke 17:21 NIV).

What would happen if we "made room" for God to do whatever He would like to do in our meetings? What would happen if we were to open and use the "eyes of our hearts" to wait in expectancy for His revelation like the disciples did on Pentecost? Would we begin to see more of the ways that God wants to move? Would we begin to experience more of what the presence of God wants to do among us? Would we experience the wonderful ways that God wants to reveal Himself through us? Remember, it's not an *emotion* that we are looking for. We are not seeking "an *experience*." Instead, we are gathering with expectancy to *experience God* and seek His face as He has commanded us to do! By doing this we *will have experiences* with Him!

Encountering God

In a presence-based community, encountering God is a primary *reason* for our gatherings. After all, this is what nearly every bible story is about! Everyone in the Bible had personal encounters with God! In accordance with scripture, our goal as the gathered Body of Christ is to experience and maintain connection with Jesus, the Head. The promise that Jesus made to be among us is not to tickle our senses or to create emotional experiences. God is among us when we gather to encounter Him! We are gathering to "abide in Him" in order to bear much fruit. We are gathering to worship as the priesthood who have been commissioned to minister to the Lord. We are gathering to thank Him, praise Him and adore Him as the Scriptures teach. We are gathering because of His promise:

> *For where two or three are gathered together in My name, I am there in the midst of them.* (Matthew 18:20 NKJV)

The early Church gathered with expectation for encounter! They knew that God would "show up" to empower and guide them in supernatural ways because that is what they were commissioned to do! The early Church reported extraordinary encounters with God during gatherings. The Spirit of God gave *supernatural guidance*:

> *While they were worshiping the Lord and fasting, the Holy Spirit said, "Set apart for me Barnabas and Saul for the work to which I have called them."* (Acts 13:2 NIV)

The Spirit of God *empowered them for witness*:

> *After they prayed, the place where they were meeting was shaken. And they were all filled with the Holy Spirit and spoke the word of God boldly.* (Acts 4:31 NIV)

The Spirit of God revealed His power by *miraculous signs*:

> *About midnight Paul and Silas were praying and singing hymns to God, and the other prisoners were listening to them. Suddenly there was such a violent earthquake that the foundations of the prison were shaken. At once all the prison doors flew open, and everyone's chains came loose.* (Acts 16:25-26 NIV)

The Spirit of God brought *supernatural healing*:

Then Ananias went to the house and entered it. Placing his hands on Saul, he said, "Brother Saul, the Lord—Jesus, who appeared to you on the road as you were coming here—has sent me so that you may see again and be filled with the Holy Spirit." Immediately, something like scales fell from Saul's eyes, and he could see again. He got up and was baptized. (Acts 9:17-18 NIV)

When we gather in Jesus's name, the promise of God is that the full expression of who God is, is among us! If God is in the room, healing is in the room. If God is in the room with us, then the God of love, the Author of life, is among us! Wisdom, healing and even transformation is in the room with us!

Our goal in gathering is to encounter God. We are there to seek His face in worship and to wait upon Him. The reason that we don't encounter God in our meetings is because we don't *expect* to encounter Him. He is always with us, but He does not override our authority. He will not push us out of the way and do what He wants because He has delegated His authority. God can only be encountered if encounter is the reason for our gathering.

This goal for encounter must begin to replace the practice of spectator Christianity in the Western world. Church has become boring! The usual goal is to keep the meeting moving with interesting and new information because, instead of encounter, the focus is to learn more about God.

Encounter with God is truly the most exciting thing that can happen at a church service, but attention must be given to learning *from* Him instead of learning *about* Him. Instead of consumers who show up with expectations to learn, presence-based community people come to encounter with God.

I believe that there are three specific practices that we can cultivate in order to experience the presence and the power of God in our personal and corporate lives. First, we must *make room* for God in our lives. Second, we must *recognize* when God is moving in our lives. Finally, we must *participate* with Him to see His purposes revealed on the earth.

Making Room for God

Another reason we don't encounter God in our meetings is "space issues." Sometimes there is not room enough for God to move. When my friend was unable to see the deer standing in my backyard, it was not because he had poor vision. It was also not because the deer were not present. The problem was that there was "no room" in my friend's thinking. He had no expectation for an encounter.

I have heard it said, "We fill our services so full that God can't get in!" That is so true. The past ten years of church development has seen a boom in megachurch growth. Small churches are emptying while larger churches are expanding. Many jealous small church pastors (I have been one of them) point out that large churches offer programs and classes and have more support for young families, childcare, etc. But is size a sign that God is in the house? Just because many people are coming, does that mean God will say to these leaders, "Well done, good and faithful servant" (Matthew 25:21 NIV)?

It is also true that the Bible shows that growth is an indication of the life and power of God at work! After all, the Church of Jesus grew by 3,000 people in one day after Pentecost. The church-growth axiom is true: "If it is living, it will grow!" It is quite true that if God shows up at the meeting, the people will also come! But is it the presence of God that is causing growth, or is it something else? Are people coming to encounter God or an hear excellent worship team? Are people coming to encounter God or to be with friends? In the twenty-first century, the size of the meeting is not an indicator of the presence of God. The focus for a presence-based community is not on the size of the gathering. Corporate and personal encounters with God happen in the company of thousands or in a small group.

The goal of a presence-based community is to encounter and partner with God, and to do this we must create room for Him. Often, small group gatherings best facilitate making room for God because "being in one accord" can be more easily accomplished. Large gather church events are designed to "inspire" and "inform" rather than provide room for an encounter with God.

Instead of giving room for listening, the goal of many services is to fill the silence. Much like television programming, silence means, in our minds, that something is wrong. Because Western minds have been habituated to hour-long programming, the Sunday service often is pared down to close after an hour. The goal for the meeting seems to be to keep people's attention on what is happening on stage. Inspiring worship, well-produced announcements and encouraging teaching dominate the seventy-minute schedule. Thankfully, God does show up even when there is little space given to seeking Him.

The goal of gathering to encounter God has shifted. There is a stark difference between the Church in Acts and the one on Main Street. In much of the Western Church there is precious little unoccupied space. Our goals for meeting must change. Our expectations for what we *want* to happen must change. If the Western Church is to become a presence-based community, we must make room mentally, emotionally and physically for the presence of God.

Recognizing God
Often when God does move in our personal lives and in events, believers are unsure how to respond or recognize it. Many Christians say that they have trouble hearing God's voice. Because believers have trouble recognizing when God moves, they often "move past" the event and only later recognize its importance.

Just like my friend looking out the window, his eyes saw what I saw, but he was unable to recognize it. I could see the deer in my backyard, but he could not. He not only had to be told to look, but also what to look for. Once he knew what he was looking for then he could recognize it when he saw it.

Leadership with the ability to equip the Church to recognize the presence of God is needed. Many times the church conducts meetings without the expectation of encounter with God. The presence of God *is* always among His people when they are gathered in His name. But training believers to "wait on" the Lord and then to recognize His move is needed. Often Christian leaders have well-trained hearts to hear God, but instead of equipping others to recognize and host the presence of God, they often continue to serve as an intermediary. This is an old covenant priesthood pattern. Now that all believers are commissioned to participate as a kingdom of priests, leaders in the

Church are not providers but leaders who equip the saints. There is a well-known proverb about provision that says, "Give someone a fish, and they will eat for a day. Teach them to fish, and they will eat for a lifetime." Servant Leaders in a presence-based community equip the saints for the priesthood ministry rather than perform it for others.

The importance of recognizing "teachable moments" in fellowship with other believers is essential. All believers should be equipped to recognize the activity of God in their lives. Taking moments to point out what God is doing is an important strategy for this. It is similar to the interaction with my friend and the deer sighting. It only took a minute to "point out" the presence of the deer in my backyard and then he was able to recognize them when he saw them move. His eyes were not trained to see, but when he was told what to look for, and he made room for understanding, then he was able to see them. This happened because I wanted him to see and experience what I was seeing.

When saints can recognize that God is present and moving among us, then they will be able to be affected by the presence of God. The presence of God *is* among His people according to the promise of Jesus when we are gathered in His name! This is the promise of God and we can be confident that God will do as He has promised. It is our responsibility to look for Him; to recognizing His move, to hear His voice and partner in His work among us. In this way, we are enabled to participate with Him.

Participation with God
God is always at work on the earth. He reveals His divine purposes on the earth when we partner with Him! The invitation to join with God in His work occurs when we recognize what He is doing. As we have discussed, agreement and partnership is the plan of God! God moves powerfully on the earth, but He has chosen to do so through people who make room for Him and agree with His revelation.

Believers partner with God not only by agreement, but also by joining with Him in His work. For example, God spoke to Moses and told him that He was going to deliver the people of God from their oppression in Egypt (Exodus 3). This revelation came with an opportunity for Moses to join with God in His work. The revelation of God to Moses was for the purpose of inviting him to participate. This is how God works on the earth to reveal His glory!

This pattern of "revelation and invitation" is consistent throughout the Bible. God revealed His plan to Noah. God told Noah that He was about to destroy the earth with a flood (Genesis 6). As a part of this revelation, Noah was invited to participate with God by building an ark. David the shepherd boy was anointed by Samuel to be king according to the move of God in Samuel's life (1 Samuel 16). This event came with a revelation that enabled David to kill Goliath, gather an army and eventually become the king of Israel.

The manifestation of the Kingdom of God on the earth occurs when Jesus's Lordship is acknowledged. Because Jesus is Lord of our lives, we make room for Him, recognize His activity in our lives, and respond to the invitations that He gives to join Him in His work. The presence of God is manifest in the love and actions of the living Body of Christ in participation with Jesus the Head.

> And **He** [Jesus] ***is the head of the body***, *the church, who is the beginning, the firstborn from the dead,* ***that in all things He may have the preeminence***. (Colossians 1:18 NKJV, emphasis added)

Jesus is revealed on the earth when we make room for Him, recognize His activity among us, and partner with Him to reveal His glory on the earth!

Chapter 9

REVEALING HIS GLORY

The Church of Jesus Christ is called to reveal His presence on the earth. Rather than impressing people with the claims of Jesus, we are called to reveal the presence of Jesus—as well as "proclaim the good news." The good news is contained in His love for all humanity. The love of God is revealed through people who reflect the presence of God. Instead of carrying a finite human love, the infinite love of God is expressed to others through the presence-based community. When evangelism is attempted without the love of God, people often respond with the same excitement as they do to telemarketing. Very few people are interested in a relationship with God if they have not seen its success in the lives of others. Teddy Roosevelt once said, "Nobody cares how much you know, until they know how much you care!"[1] This is absolutely the case with our faith.

Presence Ministry

Presence ministry is the plan of God for His people, instead of teaching people more about Jesus. The goal of the presence-based community is to reveal the presence of God. Believers are called to reveal the presence of God by being transformed into the "likeness" of God:

> *Now the Lord is the Spirit; and where the Spirit of the Lord is, there is liberty. But we all, with unveiled face, beholding as in a mirror the glory of the Lord, **are being transformed into the same image from glory to glory, just as by the Spirit of the Lord.*** (2 Corinthians 3:17-18 NKJV, emphasis added)

The original intention of God—that of being created in His image—is fulfilled in the new covenant. The Church reveals the presence of God on the earth by means of participation with His presence among them!

The early believers transformed the world because of the presence of God that was manifest among them. Tertullian, a North African Christian leader, wrote a letter to the Roman authorities in 197 A.D. that described the nature of the Church. In this letter, he described how the Christians made it their unfailing practice to care for those within the Church, and even their enemies, with great love:

> But it is mainly the deeds of a love so noble that lead many to put a brand upon us. *See*, they say, *how they love one another*, for themselves are animated by mutual hatred.[2]

No wonder the Bible tells us that "the Lord added to the church daily those who were being saved" (Acts 2:47 NKJV). Loving others must be accompanied by an explanation of the source, but the explanation will not be understood if the love of God is not present. Paul described the importance of love related to speech:

> *If I speak in the tongues of men or of angels, but do not have love, I am only a resounding gong or a clanging cymbal. If I have the gift of prophecy and can fathom all mysteries and all knowledge, and if I have a faith that can move mountains, but do not have love, I am nothing.* (1 Corinthians 13:1-2 NIV)

According to Paul, revealing the love of God to others is the validation for supernatural ministry rather than signs and wonders. Instead of proving the power of God by participating in tongues, prophecy, words of knowledge or gifts of faith, the presence-based community is called to reveal the love of God as the source of all ministry and witness. *This is presence ministry.* The example, as always, is Jesus Himself, who continually "revealed" the Father (John 17:6 NIV) to those around Him out of the overflow of His intimacy with the Father.

The second greatest commandment is "Love your neighbor as yourself" (Matthew 22:39 NIV). How will we love others in such an unselfish way? The capability to perform the second greatest commandment actually depends on our participation in the greatest one. The greatest commandment is "Love the LORD your God with all your heart, with all your soul, with all your mind, and with all your strength" (Mark 12:30 NKJV). Consider this: if we enter into a relationship with the presence of God with all that we have, then we will not be empty of love. Instead, the love of God that we experience in this relationship becomes the source of love for others. The love that we are commanded to give to others is not our own! It is the love that is cultivated in our hearts and lives by obedience to the first commandment. Paul described it this way:

> *Now hope does not disappoint, because the love of God has been*
> *poured out in our hearts by the Holy Spirit who was given to us.*
> (Romans 5:5 NKJV)

Because the love of God "has been poured out in our hearts" by fellowship with the Spirit of God, we have the capacity to love others with the love that we have received from Him. This is the *source* for presence ministry. It originates in the endless love of God that is "poured out in our hearts."

The Prayers That We Pray

The prayers that are recorded in the Bible are not for things that we today might pray for. The prayers recounted in the New Testament are not for relief from persecution. In fact, after being arrested and threatened by the Jewish leaders, the disciples met together and fervently prayed for more boldness and greater power to reveal the purposes of God on the earth:

*"Now, Lord, look on their threats, **and grant to Your servants that
with all boldness they may speak Your word, by stretching out
Your hand to heal, and that signs and wonders may be done
through the name of Your holy Servant Jesus."** And when they had
prayed, the place where they were assembled together was shaken;
and they were all filled with the Holy Spirit, and they spoke the word
of God with boldness.* (Acts 4:29-31 NKJV, emphasis added)

The disciples who prayed this prayer had just been arrested and
threatened by the religious leaders! They knew from the example of
Jesus that they would be persecuted! Instead of asking God to reduce
the resistance, they prayed for power to overcome!

Of course, believers in the new testament pray for provision, de-
liverance from trouble and the fulfillment of needs, but these are not
the only purpose for prayer. The pattern of prayer that Jesus taught
His disciples prioritizes a passionate request for the revelation of the
Kingdom of God on the earth:

*This, then, is how you should pray: "Our Father in heaven, hal-
lowed be your name, **your kingdom come, your will be done, on
earth as it is in heaven."** (Matthew 6:9-10 NIV, emphasis added)

Jesus taught His disciples to pray that God's Kingdom would be established on the earth "*as it is* in heaven"! How is God's will and Kingdom expressed in Heaven? In Heaven, the fullness of God's glory is revealed. There is no war, no death, no crying. The atmosphere of Heaven
is full of worship. Every being in Heaven can see and experience God's
wonderful love! The prayers of a presence-based community are not dependent on the desire of humans but are focused on the desire of God.
In this way, we pray in partnership with Heaven, by agreement in prayer
for the way that God desires to be revealed; we partner with Him to see
His Kingdom come and His will be done on the earth.

The New Covenant Dream
During His last hour with His disciples and just before His arrest at
midnight, Jesus prayed for Himself, for His disciples and "for those

who will believe in me through their message" (John 17:20 NIV). This prayer is recorded for us in the verses of John 17. It is the pinnacle of Scripture.

The significance of nearly every phrase in this chapter is so rich, but the heart of the prayer as it pertains to the Church is found starting at verse 20. In this passage, Jesus pours out His spirit to God regarding His deepest dreams and desires for the Church "those who will believe in Me through their word..." I have quoted the Literal Translation of the Bible because it will allow us to encounter this passage in a fresh way.

> *And I do not pray concerning these only, but also concerning* ***those who will believe in Me through their word;*** *that all may* ***be one, as You are in Me, Father, and I in You,*** *that they also* ***may be one in Us,*** *that the world may believe that You sent Me. And* ***I have given them the glory*** *which You have given Me, that* ***they may be one, as We are One: I in them, and You in Me,*** *that* ***they may be perfected in one;*** *and* ***that the world may know*** *that* ***You sent Me and loved them,*** *even as You loved Me. Father, I desire that those whom You have given Me,* ***that where I am, they may be with Me also,*** *that they may* ***see My glory which You gave Me,*** *because You loved Me before the foundation of the world. Righteous Father, indeed the world did not know You, but I knew You; and these have known that You sent Me. And* ***I made known to them Your name, and will make it known,*** *that the love with which You* ***loved Me may be in them, and I in them.*** (John 17:20-26 LITV, emphasis added)

This prayer is a passionate expression of Jesus's heart for the Church. Although this passage is so important, I have rarely heard it read or taught. For a long time, I also had trouble making sense of what, at first glance, seems to be a repetitive prayer for unity in the Church. But this prayer is not about unity among church members. This prayer is the visionary hope and petition that Jesus expressed in prayer to God for those in all ages who believe in Him. This is Jesus's prayer for us!

This new covenant prayer of Jesus is not like a prayer that you and I might pray. In many ways it seems like this prayer breaks all the rules! Jesus did not pray that we would have it easy. He did not pray that we would be victorious, stop sinning or be safe from the devil. He didn't pray that we would do miracles or evangelize. When you consider what Jesus did not pray for, what else is there?

Instead of praying *for* anything, Jesus revealed His heart's cry, the dream in His heart for the revelation of the fullness God in the Church. He prayed that the Church would experience oneness with God in the same way that He experienced it. He prayed for four primary relational objectives. These relational objectives are critical to *everything* in presence-based community. Jesus prayed for:

Oneness—that we would be one with God.

Glory—that we would reveal the glory of God.

To know God—that we would maintain vital connection with God.

To make Him known—that we would reveal the presence of God to the world.

Oneness with God

Jesus prayed "that all of them may be one, Father, just as you are in me and I am in you. May they also be in us..." (John 17:21 NIV). Jesus was not praying for the unity of the Church. Instead, He was praying for the Church to experience the same *oneness* with the Father that He experienced. Jesus is praying for intimacy and unity with the presence of God, not cooperation between church members! The original word that is often translated as "unity" has nothing to do with cooperation. Instead, it is the same word that Jesus used in describing His relationship with the Father. Jesus told the Pharisees, "I and the Father are one" (John 10:30 NIV). By this statement, Jesus simply meant that there was no separation between His life and the life of God. Jesus was passionately praying that His followers would experience the same "oneness" in relationship with God that was continually His!

Revealing His Glory

The word that is translated as "glory" actually means "fullness or weightiness."[3] While the word *glory* most often refers to the "glory of God" in the Bible, it can and is used to describe other things: "the glory of his riches..." (Esther 5:11 NASB), "the glory of young men..." (Proverbs 20:29 NASB), and "the glory of his forest..." (Isaiah 10:18 NASB).

Jesus prayed, "I have given them the glory [fullness] that you gave me" (John 17:22 NIV). Then He prayed that we would see the glory (fullness) that the Father gave to Him (John 17:24). Instead of halos (or whatever we used to think that glory was), the dream of Jesus for us is that we would experience the *fullness* of God in our lives! He is praying that we would live and operate with the same fullness that *He experienced,* lived and operated in during His life and ministry! Imagine that! Jesus was praying that we would experience and reveal the same passionate love, proclaim the same powerful teaching, perform the same astonishing miracles, and do it all with the same purpose and power that He did!

Knowing God and Making Him Known

Finally, Jesus continued His prayer by stating, "I have made known to them Your name, and will make it known..." (John 17:26 LITV). Jesus was declaring that He was going to make the fullness of God known to us and that He would continue to make Himself known! This is an extension of the promise He made to His disciples:

> *No longer do I call you servants, for a servant does not know what his master is doing; but I have called you friends, for **all things that I heard from My Father I have made known to you**.* (John 15:15 NKJV, emphasis added)

Jesus was perpetuating the promise that He gave to His disciples. Instead of acting like a master whose servants don't know what he is thinking, Jesus promised to reveal all that was in His heart, just like He did for the first disciples.

No other spiritual community would look like this! Jesus was not establishing a religious order based on His teachings. Instead, Jesus was establishing a presence-based community that existed in relationship and ongoing knowledge of the plans and purposes of God!

Manifestation of the Spirit

Jesus revealed the fullness of God by miracles, signs and wonders. Jesus also promised that all those who believe would do the same:

> *Very truly I tell you, whoever believes in me will do the works I have been doing, and they will do even greater things than these, because I am going to the Father.* (John 14:12 NIV)

The original word that is translated as "believe" in this passage does not mean "acknowledge the existence of." Rather, it means "entrust" or "to trust in."[4] So, the true meaning of this verse is something like this: "Whoever puts their trust in Me will do the very works that I have been doing…and they will do even greater things than these." This verse is amazing! The entire repertoire of works that Jesus performed—and greater—will be done by those who trust in Him! Because of this, we continue to pray for the sick and minister according to the pattern of Jesus.

It is important to admit at this point that we have not seen the fullness of this promise in our ministry for every situation. We have seen God do miracles. We regularly see God heal and transform people by His Spirit, but the fullness of the promise of Jesus for doing what He did and even greater is not yet a reality among us. It is not happening yet, but it will.

The culture of doubt and limitation that believers have placed on the capacity of the presence of God among us to transform and create supernatural change among us is crumbling. Instead of compromising our trust in the promise of God to correspond with our past experience, we must choose to enter into partnership with God like children trusting a good Father. Trusting God to fulfill His promise is what enabled all of the patriarchs of the Bible to see God move on their behalf:

> *Now faith is confidence in what we hope for and assurance about what we do not see. This is what the ancients were commended for.* (Hebrews 11:1-2 NIV)

Followers of Jesus must not amend the promises of God to agree with past experiences. Instead, we must choose to trust in

God according to what He has promised. In this way we will obtain an assurance of what we do not yet see. This agreement with God is necessary for the fullness of His revelation on the earth. Instead of avoiding any statements of belief, we must choose to say, "Lord, I believe; help my unbelief" (Mark 9:24 NKJV)! Instead of lowering our faith to the level of our past experiences, we must decide instead to agree with God in order to experience the fullness of the promises that He has given to us. I have seen God fulfill His Word so many times but experiencing God's work among us is rarely a process of seeing and *then* believing. Partnership with God is agreement with His plan and then seeing it happen. This is called faith:

> *So then faith comes by hearing, and hearing by the word of God.*
> (Romans 10:17 NKJV)

A presence-based community is a community of faith. Hearing God is the first step in the sequence of biblical faith. In yielded partnership with God, the revelation of His glory is initiated by hearing God and being confident in God to fulfill His Word. This is faith. It cannot rest on what *each person wants* God to do. The revelation of the glory of God on the earth starts with hearing His voice and agreeing with what *He wants* to do. This is how we live in such a manner to reveal the glory of God on the earth. God fulfills all of His promises. In partnership with God we will continue to experience the promises of the new covenant for us along with all who believe!

Manifestation Gifts
The revelation of God's glory on the earth is accomplished by people who are yielded in partnership with the Spirit of God. Love is the source and prerequisite for all supernatural manifestation. Within the presence-based community, God has chosen to enable *each* member of the Body of Christ to minister *His* grace to others. The grace of God in all of its variety of expressions is distributed to each member according to *His* will. Paul wrote:

We have different gifts, according to the grace given to each of us... (Romans 12:6 NIV)

This use of the word *gift* is found over twenty-five times in the New Testament and is a form of the root word "grace." The word translated as "gift" in these passages actually means "endowment."[5] One way of understanding these endowments is to see them as "grace gifts" that God imparts to His people in order for them to encourage one another. Instead of gifts that believers use for their own benefit, these gifts are given to each believer to be "managed" or "stewarded" as ministry to encourage others. Peter described this in his letter:

Each of you should use whatever gift you have received to serve others, as faithful stewards of God's grace in its various forms. (1 Peter 4:10 NIV)

The use of these grace gifts can only be properly accomplished by participation with the Spirit to love and encourage other believers. Just like the parable of the master giving charge of his fortune to his servants, God is looking for people who properly "put to use" the gifts that are given to them.

There are different kinds of supernatural "graces" or gifts that the Spirit of God distributes to each believer who is yielded to Him. Paul listed and gave some brief information about nine of them:

*Now about the gifts of the Spirit, brothers and sisters, I do not want you to be uninformed... There are different **kinds** of gifts, but the same Spirit distributes them. There are different **kinds of service**, but the same Lord. There are different **kinds of working**, but in all of them and in everyone it is the same God at work. Now **to each one the manifestation of the Spirit is given for the common good**. To one there is given through the Spirit a **message of wisdom**, to another a **message of knowledge** by means of the same Spirit, to another **faith** by the same Spirit, to another **gifts of healing** by that one Spirit, to another **miraculous powers**, to another **prophecy**, to another **distinguishing between*** *spirits,* to another **speaking in different kinds of tongues,** and to still another the **interpretation of tongues.** All these are the work of one and the same Spirit, and **he distributes them to each one, just as he determines.** (1 Corinthians 12:1,4-11 NIV, emphasis added)

In English translations of this passage, the word *gift* has been added to the introductory verse. English translations read, "Now concerning spiritual *gifts,* I do not want you to be ignorant" (1 Corinthians 12:1 NKJV). The word *gift,* however, is *not* in the original language. More correctly translated, this verse could read, "Now concerning spiritual things, I do not want you to be ignorant." This is important. The proper meaning of this introduction is to indicate that this is the way God spiritually works among us. It is not about spiritual tools that the Spirit gives to put in our toolbox. It is not a list of things that can happen during a church service. Instead, Paul's intention was to instruct the Corinthian believers about the spiritual way that the presence of God works through each believer using the grace gifts.

The nine grace gifts listed in this passage are commonly called the "manifestational gifts." The description of the *three forms* and *one purpose* of these grace gifts is found in verses 4 to 7.

The spiritual ministry of the grace gifts of God has *three different forms.* First, there are *different grace gifts* that are distributed by the Spirit of God. Second, there are *different types of ministries* that these grace gifts perform. Finally, there are a *variety of ways* that the Spirit works through these grace gifts.

Paul revealed the unique *purpose* of the grace gifts. The purpose of the spiritual ministry of these grace gifts is *the manifestation of the Spirit* for the benefit of everyone. The focus is not to be on the gifts themselves; their purpose is for the ongoing manifestation of the Spirit among the people of God! This changes the importance of this passage. Rather than being a passage about how each person has unique talents to be used to help others, this passage is about how the presence of God performs the spiritual ministry through each member of the Body of Christ. This passage describes the different *kinds, types* and *ways* that the grace gifts function to reveal the ministry of the Spirit of God among us!

There is one more verse that describes the distribution of the grace gifts. This is very important for our understanding so that we know how to receive them. According to verse 11 (NIV), the grace giftings are distributed to *each person*, "just as *He* determines." This means that the Spirit of God gives a grace gift to *everyone*. He also does this according to His determination. Every yielded follower of Jesus has been given gifts of grace so that he or she can participate in spiritual ministry—not just gifted leaders! As the priesthood purchased by the blood of Jesus, every yielded member of the Body is enabled by the presence of God, just as He determines, to provide spiritual ministry to the other members. The goals of this ministry is the spiritual trans- formation of members and the manifestation of the presence of God in the Church.

The grace gifts have been misunderstood. During the Charismatic Renewal of the 1960s and 70s, the gifts of the Spirit were often seen as *events* that took place during a meeting. At these events, one member ministered with a prophecy, another member presented a word of wis- dom, and many people spoke in tongues. The biblical intention of the grace gifts, however, is the *ongoing* mutual ministry of the Church— not only in a the large group gathering, but to one-to-another in all gatherings where two or three meet in His name. In this way the Ro- mans 12 passage makes sense; the presence of God becomes manifest by *various kinds* of gifts, by *various types* of ministries and in *various ways*. There is nothing wrong with grace gift ministry during meet- ings, of course. But the intention of God is to reveal His presence in spiritual ministry in every aspect of community life. *Each member* of the body of Christ is enabled to build up others using the grace gift that God has given him or her as an ongoing way to serve others.

The grace gifts are important for the function of a presence-based community. Each member must be a faithful steward of each of the giftings that he or she has received so that the Spirit of God can en- courage others in the community.

The message or word of wisdom is specific wisdom from the Spirit for another person. It is not a biblical teaching. Rather, it is specific wisdom that gives understanding to what is going on, of what to do, etc. An example can be found in Acts:

It seemed good to the Holy Spirit and to us not to burden you with anything beyond the following requirements (Acts 15:28 NIV).

The message or word of knowledge is specific information from the Spirit of God for others. The Spirit of God gives specific information to one person for another. This is demonstrated in the word of knowledge that Agabus gave to Paul:

Coming over to us, he took Paul's belt, tied his own hands and feet with it and said, "The Holy Spirit says, 'In this way the Jewish leaders in Jerusalem will bind the owner of this belt and will hand him over to the Gentiles.'" (Acts 21:11 NIV)

A gift of faith is the knowledge of the will of God before it happens. In situations where the will of God is unknown, God gives the gift of faith to individuals so that they can minister, pray and act in confidence *knowing* what God intends to do. A biblical example is Noah building an ark "by faith," even when there was no rain.

A grace gift of healing is a manifestation of the Spirit of God to heal the body, mind and spirit. Through the ministry of one person, by prayer or declaration, the presence of God touches a person and brings health. This gift was one of the hallmarks of the ministry of Jesus and the early Church.

Miraculous powers are literally paranormal manifestations of the Spirit of God. In these situations, the Spirit of God moves through individuals to physically or emotionally create change. Philip experienced this when he was ministering to the Ethiopian eunuch:

Now when they came up out of the water, the Spirit of the Lord caught Philip away, so that the eunuch saw him no more; and he went on his way rejoicing. But Philip was found at Azotus. And passing through, he preached in all the cities till he came to Caesarea. (Acts 8:39-40 NKJV)

Prophecy is a declaration of God's intention through one person to others. Peter described the nature of prophecy:

For prophecy never had its origin in the human will, but prophets, though human, spoke from God as they were carried along by the Holy Spirit. (2 Peter 1:21 NIV)

The gift of distinguishing between spirits is a grace gift from the Spirit of God that enables a yielded follower of Jesus to discern the spiritual source of words or actions. Paul demonstrated this understanding and responded to the spiritual source of a servant girl's disturbing behavior:

Now it happened, as we went to prayer, that a certain slave girl possessed with a spirit of divination met us, who brought her masters much profit by fortune-telling. This girl followed Paul and us, and cried out, saying, "These men are the servants of the Most High God, who proclaim to us the way of salvation." And this she did for many days. But Paul, greatly annoyed, turned and said to the spirit, "I command you in the name of Jesus Christ to come out of her." And he came out that very hour. (Acts 16:16-18 NKJV)

Tongues is a supernatural grace gifting that is common to nearly all believers in the New Testament. All of the 120 people and the apostles gathered at Pentecost spoke in tongues. Paul described the function of the manifestation of tongues in the life of the believer:

For anyone who speaks in a tongue does not speak to people but to God. Indeed, no one understands them; they utter mysteries by the Spirit. (1 Corinthians 14:2 NIV)

The interpretation of tongues occurs in the gathering of believers to encourage them. Public declaration given in unintelligible tongue by one member is followed by an intelligible interpretation so that not just one person, but all can understand and be encouraged by the declaration.

So it is with you. Since you are eager for gifts of the Spirit, try to excel in those that build up the church. For this reason the one who speaks in a tongue should pray that they may interpret what they say. For if I pray in a tongue, my spirit prays, but my mind is unfruitful. (1 Corinthians 14:12-14 NIV)

Members of the presence-based community are commissioned and empowered to humbly reveal the fullness of God's presence on the earth. When God's glory is revealed through the presence-based community, the new covenant dream of Jesus is realized on the earth:

That they all may be one, as You, Father, are in Me, and I in You; that they also may be one in Us, that the world may believe that You sent Me. (John 17:21 NKJV)

Chapter Ten
THE
KINGDOM
OF GOD

The Kingdom of God exists wherever God reigns. In the Kingdom of God there is only one sovereign King and many subjects. Countless saints are under His reign; some are in Heaven and some are here on the earth. Members of God's Kingdom include the seraphim, the cherubim and a host of ancient angels. The Kingdom of God can exist inside of one person; it can exist in a group of people; or it can (and will eventually) cover the earth "as the waters cover the sea" (Isaiah 11:9 NKJV).

The Kingdom of God is not a democracy. God is sovereign and does what He wants without limitation or regulation. He responds only to the limits that He has placed upon Himself. But all God does is good, so whatever He wants is good! Even so, the concept of sovereignty is repulsive to most Westerners. It is hard for us to imagine that God would not be corrupted by His sovereign power because humans who gain sovereignty are nearly always given to corruption. Our suspicion of God has created quite a hurdle for us. However, membership in the Kingdom of God means that Love reigns. There is no need for rebellion or impeachment. The only choice we are given is rebellion that leads to death or partnership that leads to love!

Jesus taught about the Kingdom of God more than any other subject. Over eighty times in Scripture, Jesus described what the reign of God looks like. Revealing the nature of the Kingdom of God was the primary focus of Jesus's life and ministry.

Jesus wanted us to know what the reign of God looks like. He described what God intended to do by saying, "The kingdom of God is like..." (e.g., Mark 4:30). According to Jesus in Matthew 13, the Kingdom of God is like a treasure hidden in the field. It is like a merchant looking for the one pearl of great price. The Kingdom of God is like a sower who sowed good seed in his field. These amazing parables are invaluable to understanding how God works on the earth through His presence-based community.

Jesus told Pilate that His Kingdom was "not of this world" (John 18:36 NIV). But the Kingdom of God is not *only* in Heaven. It is a spiritual realm that *begins* in Heaven and extends to earth. It is on the earth whenever people partner with God. It is a real spiritual Kingdom.

Jesus taught that His Kingdom is not discovered by the powers of human observation:

> ...*Jesus replied, "The Kingdom of God **can't be detected by visible signs**. You won't be able to say, 'Here it is!' or 'It's over there!' For the Kingdom of God is already among you."* (Luke 17:20-21 NLT, emphasis added)

The reign of God does not suddenly materialize in one place or another; nor is it just a state of mind. The Kingdom of God is a supernatural realm that can and does already exist on the earth. It is enabled and perpetuated by those who live under the Lordship of Jesus, by those who live in righteous relationship with God and others. Thus, the Kingdom of God is *within* and *among* His presence-based community.

The Kingdom of God is not a religious sect. It is not *defined* by a set of rituals, ethics or culture. It is centered in the presence of God, but it exists as an exciting corporate reality under the Lordship of Jesus

Christ. No one ruler on the earth can possess the Kingdom of God. Instead, it is the possession of those who are aliens and foreigners among the kingdoms of the earth. But the citizens of the Kingdom of Heaven are excellent earthly citizens. Those who are of this Kingdom walk with honor and integrity toward earthly governments but with a primary allegiance in Heaven.

Jesus taught His disciples to pray that the Kingdom of God would come to earth and that God's will would be done on earth, just as it is in Heaven (Matthew 6:10). Jesus taught His disciples that the Kingdom of God is "forcefully advancing" on the earth. Instead of attempting to redirect or resist the coming Kingdom, we are invited to "lay hold of it" and participate in it (Matthew 11:12 NKJV). The aim of the presence-based community is zealous apprehension of the reign of God on the earth!

The Wineskin

At the beginning of Jesus's ministry, the religious leaders began to question His methods. Jesus did not teach His disciples to fast; He ate with sinners; and He taught His disciples to call God, "Father." At one point, Jesus used an illustration from everyday life to describe how the Kingdom that He was bringing was affecting the earthly kingdom. He talked about wineskins:

> *He told them this parable: "No one tears a piece out of a new garment to patch an old one. Otherwise, they will have torn the new garment, and the patch from the new will not match the old. And no one pours new wine into old wineskins. Otherwise, the new wine will burst the skins; the wine will run out and the wineskins will be ruined. No, new wine must be poured into new wineskins. And no one after drinking old wine wants the new, for they say, 'The old is better.'"* (Luke 5:36-39 NIV)

This is a very important passage for understanding the Kingdom of God. The unfortunate thing about this illustration is that we no longer use wineskins. In fact, most people don't even know what a wineskin is! The important and relevant meaning that was so accessible to the hearers of this illustration in Jesus's day is hidden to us. To understand what Jesus was saying, we first need to know about the way that wine was processed and stored in the first century.

In Jesus's day there were no bottles for storing wine. Instead, when a goat was butchered, the skin was removed and the hide processed so that it could be fabricated into an airtight container for storing wine: a wineskin. In the fall, grapes were placed in the winepress, and the grape juice was collected and placed inside of the wineskin. The wineskin was sealed so that no air could get in. This airtight wineskin was hung from the ceiling of the home while the wine fermented. During the fermentation process, the wine expanded; as a result, the wineskin became tight and hard. The wineskin retained its rigidity even when the wine was poured out for use. One end of the rigid wineskin was opened, and it could be used to carry water, etc. However, the old wineskin could not be reused as an airtight container for wine a second time due to its rigidity. If new wine was placed inside the old wineskin and the end sewn shut, the pressure of the fermentation process would cause the wineskin to burst. The wine would be lost, and the old wineskin would no longer be valuable for carrying water, etc.

Jesus was using this illustration to describe the relationship between "structure" and "life" in the Kingdom of God. He was describing the devastating consequences of attempting to contain the "life" (the new wine) of the new covenant within the "structure" (the wineskin) of the old covenant. In the end, Jesus was warning, that if the "life" of the new covenant was placed within the confines of the old, then the value of both would be lost.

The power and the purposes of the new covenant that Jesus revealed to the world cannot be contained in the structures of the old covenant. The new covenant community redeemed by the blood of Jesus could not be contained within a covenant that was mediated by animal sacrifice and temple worship. The veil was torn! A new structure was needed for the new covenant. This did not mean that there would be no structure, no organization. Without a structure, the new wine would be lost. Instead, a new wineskin that would support the purposes and the power of the new covenant was needed. A structure that would allow room for the "life" of God to flourish was needed.

The new covenant would need to exist within a dynamic structure that would support the new life and not restrict it!

Structures That Support Life

The wineskin also becomes an illustration of how the structure of the Church must not remain static but be flexible and capable of supporting the dynamic life within the Church. Just like a flexible wineskin must be used for the new wine, so it is essential that the structure of what God is doing be supported by structures that do not limit its purpose and power. In a presence-based community, we have a phrase that helps us determine the value of traditions within the structure of the Church. We call it "structures that support life." Programs and traditions are wonderful. God uses them as structures that enable the life of the presence-based community to flourish. But structures that inhibit the life of God in a presence-based community must be evaluated according to discernment. Instead of perpetuating programs and systems within the local expression of the Church that restrict and resist what the Spirit of God is doing, we must evaluate the "wineskin" from time to time. Meaningful traditions that support the life and history of God among a presence-based community are maintained while structures that inhibit the presence of God are laid to rest. Many of the traditions practiced by the Church fifty years ago are not able to support the expression of a presence-based community. Ongoing discernment about the benefit of these programs and traditions must be a function of a presence-based community.

The principles and practices of a presence-based community are the same as they were when Jesus instituted them nearly 2,000 years ago, but the cultural and relevant structures that support these principles and practices change slowly over time. Rather than supporting rigid structures, it is important that the structures support and enable the life of the presence-based community. In our discernment about "how to do" a presence-based community, it is important to examine the practices that Jesus employed and the structure of the early Church.

The Four Devotions

After Pentecost, a core group of 120 believers and those from the 3,000 who responded to Peter's invitation gathered as the first presence-based community. The New Testament reveals that this was a time of amazing growth and incredible excitement. "Life" was happening everywhere. But just like new wine that was being produced, a structure to support and encourage the life was also needed so that the life was not lost.

So, what was the structure of the early Church? How did the early Church contain all the new growth and continue to experience the presence of God now that there were thousands of people? Fortunately, there is a fairly specific description of the principles that guided the life of the early Church in the Book of Acts:

> They devoted themselves to the **apostles' teaching** and to **fellowship**, to the **breaking of bread** and to **prayer**. Everyone was filled with awe at the many wonders and signs performed by the apostles. All the believers were together and had everything in common. They sold property and possessions to give to anyone who had need. Every day they continued to meet together in the temple courts. They broke bread in their homes and ate together with glad and sincere hearts, praising God and enjoying the favor of all the people. And the Lord added to their number daily those who were being saved. (Acts 2:42-47 NIV)

During this period of fantastic growth, it was not structure that formed the life of the Church. Instead of focusing on containing and controlling the practices of the presence-based community, the format of their gatherings were guided by four practices. These four "devotions" were the basis for maintenance of the life and vision of the Church. These four devotions continued to maintain the growth and the focus of the first presence-based community based on the first and second great commandments.

The word *devoted* means "constantly diligent."[1] Rather than following a program of study or maintaining an effort to obey laws, the early Church was "constantly diligent" to practice four specific activities that became the nexus of life for everything that the presence of God would do among them.

Apostles' Teaching: The Word of God

The early believers were devoted to the teaching of the twelve disciples who they called apostles. People gathered in large and small groups to learn from those who had been with Jesus. There were no Bibles! The Word of God was being transferred to all of the new disciples by the testimony of the twelve apostles. This knowledge of Jesus's words and the principles that the disciples taught from the Lord became the basis for a knowledge of what was important for the first presence-based community.

This devotion to the Word of God was a second commandment devotion. Encouragement and discipleship in the Word of God was a way of ministering to one another.

Fellowship: Non-Optional Relationships

The second devotion that this passage described is "devotion to fellowship." Most Western believers equate the word *fellowship* with the idea of getting together with other believers for a meal. While fellowship often does happen when members of the presence-based community gather, the true meaning of the original word translated as "fellowship" in this passage actually comes from a root word meaning "having in common."[2] This word does not only mean "enjoying one another's company"; it also connotes interdependence—lives that are lived in connection to one another. The first-century members of this presence-based community joined together to love and care for one another. They used their gifts to minister one to another and pray for one another. They chose to support one another and serve one another. They shared their possessions, and if someone was in need, they gave out of their resources to assist that person. Rather than living independently, they lived in *non-optional relationships* with each other in which they relied on one another for everything. Non-optional relationships seem quite foreign to fiercely independent Westerners. Learning to lay aside patterns of rugged individuality will be difficult for nations that have been formed by a spirit of independence that values "life, liberty and the pursuit of happiness."

This devotion to caring for one another was also a second commandment expression. Fellowship is certainly an expression of the command of Jesus to "love one another."

Breaking of Bread: Worship

The first-century Church gathered regularly—if not daily, then at least weekly—for the Lord's supper. The Bible states that the believers gathered for worship not just on the Lord's day (Acts 13:2; 16:25). Believers gathered to adore Jesus by receiving the bread and the cup as well as singing and giving thanks to God. The first presence-based community was devoted to these worship gatherings. Gathering to worship and celebrate the Lord's supper was a way of drawing close to the presence of Jesus.

Worship was a first commandment devotion. By gathering to give praise and honor to Jesus, they were participating in the command to love God with all their heart, soul, mind and strength!

Prayer: Listening and Speaking

The early Church was truly devoted to prayer. Instead of praying before the meeting, praying *was* the meeting! The first presence-based community gathered regularly in homes and in large groups for prayer. The primary gatherings took place in the morning at sunrise and in the evening at sunset. Rather than asking God for things, this early prayer consisted of periods of stillness, of waiting on the Lord. The method of communication was not one way, but it began with listening and then responding to the Lord.

Prayer is a first commandment devotion. Gathering to listen, respond and wait on the Lord surely is a way to love God with all of one's heart, soul, mind and strength!

Meetings

A presence-based community is a society based on these four devotions. Rather than a weekly meeting, a presence-based community is the society of believers who gather on a regular basis for the purpose of encountering God. The practices of these four devotions provide purpose and power to become a transformed society.

The practice of these four devotions in yielded partnership with the presence of God provided direction and power for the many signs, wonders and miracles they experienced. Instead of meeting weekly for an hour service, the early Church met spontaneously and often. They met in small groups in homes and in large groups in the temple courts for the purpose of worship and encounter with God. Because of these four devotions, they were joined in fellowship with God and each other. The presence of God was manifest in incredible ways.

They met as a large group in the temple courts on the first day of the week. In small groups, they met daily in homes. The Bible says that these meetings were marked by sincerity and gladness (Acts 2:46). They enjoyed eating together. The results of these four devotions are amazing. The first presence-based community enjoyed the love and favor of those who surrounded them, and *daily* people were giving their lives to Jesus and joining with the new society of Jesus lovers.

House to House
For the first 300 years, the Church existed without any buildings. During this time, the Church met in homes or in public places. Home group meetings were not *only* a weekly event; often the gathering of two to three people was for the purpose of prayer or to encourage one another. These meetings were not secondary meetings but were actually the primary meetings of the Church for almost 400 years. Consider what Paul wrote in his greeting to Philemon:

> *Paul, a prisoner of Christ Jesus, and Timothy our brother, to Philemon our dear friend and fellow worker—also to Apphia our sister and Archippus our fellow soldier—and **to the church that meets in your home**.* (Philemon 1-2 NIV, emphasis added)

Paul was asking that his greeting be delivered to the church that met in Philemon's home! Could it be that when the writers of the New Testament wrote about "the churches," they were referencing these home groups? Yes! There were no church buildings until the fourth century! The church meeting *was* a home group for the first 300 years of the Church!

Paul described what one of these home group meetings was like in his first letter to the Corinthians:

> *What then shall we say, brothers and sisters? When you come together, each of you has a hymn, or a word of instruction, a revelation, a tongue or an interpretation. Everything must be*

done so that the church may be built up. If anyone speaks in a tongue, two—or at the most three—should speak, one at a time, and someone must interpret. If there is no interpreter, the speaker should keep quiet in the church and speak to himself and to God. Two or three prophets should speak, and the others should weigh carefully what is said. And if a revelation comes to someone who is sitting down, the first speaker should stop. For you can all prophesy in turn so that everyone may be instructed and encouraged. (1 Corinthians 14:26-31 NIV)

In this meeting, we see that many members are participating. One person leads a hymn, another brings a word of instruction, another speaks a "revelation," and still another speaks in tongues or brings an interpretation. Several people prophesy while the others are encouraged to discern what is being said. The important thing to notice is that the focus of the meeting is on building one another up. Rather than one person leading, we see that mutual ministry plays a huge part. Instead of one person providing expert teaching or priestly guidance, several people in the group participate in the ministry of instruction and encouragement. This is a confirmation of the use of the grace gifts in First Corinthians 12.

The Bible uses the word *edification* to describe the goal of mutual ministry. Edification means to "build up."[3] Edification is the primary way that members in a presence-based community minister to one another.

Let us therefore make every effort to do what leads to peace and to mutual edification. (Romans 14:19 NIV)

God is restoring the function of the house-to-house ministry and mutual edification that was practiced in the early Church! Stadium events are encouraging, but the Bible reveals that the life of the Church occurs in face-to-face communion.

Large Group Gatherings

In the book, *2,000 Years of Christ's Power*, N.R. Needham describes a fairly typical large group meeting in the year 120 C.E. The service often lasted three to four hours. It took place on the first day of the week and consisted of three parts.

The first part of the service was open to anyone in the community and was often called "the service of the word." During this first hour, various leaders of the Church would lead out in prayer, worship songs and Scripture reading, culminating in a sermon by the senior leader of the group, often an elder or bishop. Following the sermon, *all but* baptized believers were dismissed.

The second hour of service was for prayer. Only believers who had been baptized could participate. The elder leading the meeting would give the direction for prayer. Silent and spoken prayers from the congregation followed. This was the lengthy part of the service. Often these times of congregational prayer would last several hours. Devotional prayers, intercession and petitions were offered based on the direction of the Spirit of God.

The third part of the service was the Lord's supper. This often consisted of a period for the confession of sin. Church members brought their own small loaf of bread and flask of wine from home. The deacons took the bread, spread the loaves out on the Lord's table, and emptied the flasks of wine into one large silver cup. After communion, any unconsumed bread and wine were taken home by church members to use for celebrating communion at home during the week.[4]

Many large group meetings similar to this can be experienced in countries around the world. (I have been involved in events similar to this in China.) The mentality that persists in Western culture, however, "chafes" at a meeting like this. The goal of most Western worship services is to fulfill the needs of those gathered. Meetings that are 70 to 90 minutes long are considered sufficient. Some church growth resources report that *any* event lasting longer than 70 minutes is too long for the attention span of Americans who have been conditioned by hour long TV programming. I disagree! I have been to several music festivals in the United States where thousands of people gather. At these events, people sit for many hours day after day to listen to music! This makes perfect sense to me. The goal of these events is not only entertainment. The primary goal is encounter! People are enlivened by when they gather with friends to have corporate encounters with exciting live music. I have seen people of all ages sit for hours participating with incredible interest. Often, when these events are over, people report that the rest of their life seems boring. Active participation with other people in order to experience a meaningful shared event is not boring. It is an adventure!

At this time, God is beginning to equip the Church to once again facilitate meetings that enable the saints to actively engage in corporate encounter with God in worship, waiting, prayer and proclamation. When the presence of God shows up at a meeting, the people will also show up too! The presence of God is not boring! This was the church growth strategy of the early Church.

Servant Leaders

Leaders of a presence-based community serve the church by leading the people in the example of Jesus. A presence-based community is led by elders, according to the New Testament:

> *Paul and Barnabas appointed elders for them in each church and, with prayer and fasting, committed them to the Lord, in whom they had put their trust.* (Act 14:23 NIV)

The word *elder* in this passage means "senior"[5] and refers to someone who is mature in knowing and following the Lord. These elders were commissioned to "direct the affairs of the church":

> *The elders who direct the affairs of the church well are worthy of double honor, especially those whose work is preaching and teaching.* (1 Timothy 5:17 NIV)

Notice in this passage that some of them did preach and teach, but the function of these leaders was to serve the church by leading.

An elder could not be a person who did not serve others. The criteria for elders is quite rigorous:

> *An elder must be blameless, faithful to his wife, a man whose children believe and are not open to the charge of being wild and disobedient. Since an overseer **manages God's household**, he must be blameless—not overbearing, not quick-tempered, not given to*

*drunkenness, not violent, not pursuing dishonest gain. Rather, he must be hospitable, one who loves what is good, who is self-controlled, upright, holy and disciplined. He must **hold firmly to the trustworthy message as it has been taught,** so that he can **encourage others by sound doctrine** and **refute those who oppose it.*** (Titus 1:6-9 NIV, emphasis added)

According to this passage, elders were charged with managing the household of God. In order to do this properly, they were to demonstrate the character of Christ: blameless, not overbearing, self-controlled, not violent, not dishonest, hospitable, lover of what is good, upright, holy and disciplined. The three main responsibilities are one, to hold firmly to the message (Word of God); two, to encourage others by sound doctrine; and three, to refute those who oppose sound doctrine.

In a presence-based community, leaders of the church must be blameless servants who lead by serving. They lead the church lovingly and carefully using discernment like Jesus did. Rather than leading by popular vote, presence-based leaders lead according to the Word of God. They encourage others according to what is right, and they correct those who oppose the truth. They are strong and compassionate. Rather than doing all the ministry, an elder enables and facilitates the ministry. The elder follows the example of Jesus by discipling and equipping others to lead.

Deacons are ministry leaders in a church. The word *deacon* in the New Testament means "servant."[6] The requirements for a deacon are also listed in the New Testament:

In the same way, deacons are to be worthy of respect, sincere, not indulging in much wine, and not pursuing dishonest gain. They must keep hold of the deep truths of the faith with a clear conscience. They must first be tested; and then if there is nothing against them, let them serve as deacons. In the same way, the women are to be worthy of respect, not malicious talkers but temperate and trustworthy in everything. A deacon must be faithful to his wife and must manage his children and his household well. Those who have served well gain an excellent standing and great assurance in their faith in Christ Jesus. (1 Timothy 3:8-13 NIV)

Once again, the most important thing about leaders in a presence-based community is that they exemplify the character of Jesus. As you can see, both men and women can participate in ministry leadership as deacons. Deacons are humble men and women who serve their church by leading the mutual care ministry in the church.

Ministry leadership in a presence-based community is based on these biblical models. It is important to affirm leaders who qualify themselves according to the criteria in Scripture. These leaders are enabled to lead and are supported by members according to their needs (1 Timothy 5:17-18; 1 Corinthians 9:9-14).

Equipping the Saints
Apostles, prophets, evangelists, pastors and teachers are identified as those whom Jesus has "given" to the Church as equippers. Those who are given these designations or leadership roles are not yoked with the continuous performance of these ministries. Instead, they are called by Jesus to *equip the saints* for the work of ministry. Paul described five leadership callings in Ephesians 4:

> *And He Himself gave some to be **apostles**, some **prophets**, some **evangelists**, and some **pastors** and **teachers**, for the **equipping of the saints for the work of ministry**, for the **edifying of the body of Christ**, till we all come to the unity* ["oneness"] *of the faith and of the knowledge of the Son of God, to a perfect man, to the measure of the stature of the fullness of Christ; **that we should no longer be children, tossed to and fro** and carried about with every wind of doctrine, by the trickery of men, in the cunning craftiness of deceitful plotting, but, **speaking the truth in love**, may grow up in all things into Him who is the head—Christ—from whom the whole body, joined and knit together by what every joint supplies, according to the effective working by which every part does its share, causes growth of the body for the edifying of itself in love.* (Ephesians 4:11-16 NKJV, emphasis added)

According to this passage, the fivefold equipping ministry exists to *equip the saints* and *build up the Body of Christ*. The purpose is to bring everyone into "oneness" of faith and in a deeper knowledge of Jesus. The plan is to "perfect" the saints and to build them up until they are fully mature and transformed into the likeness of Jesus. Then immature believers will not be deceived and "blown around" by false doctrine. This work of equipping is done by "speaking the truth in love" and allowing each member to grow up in the effective work that they have been given by God. Instead of conforming each member to a single mold or standard, the goal becomes to equip them according to the purposes of God in their lives.

A Proposal
Presence-Based Community is a proposal for living in God's original purpose for the Church. In order to live in this incredible life-giving plan of God, there must be a radical reordering of focus and priority.

This book is a proposal for the Church—a proposal for encounter and engagement with the presence of God. Instead of gathering to learn about God, we must gather to learn from God. The Church must respond with yieldedness in relationship in order to experience the desire of God to live among His people. It is a proposal for a radical return to the new covenant example and teachings of Jesus and the early Church—to live by abiding in Him. It is a call to be a true community defined by mutual love and care for one another in order to reveal the presence of God on the earth.

Presence-based community is about living in the full expression of the Church that Jesus died for! It is a call to live as a kingdom of priests—believers who minister to God as a primary occupation and reign by partnering with Him on the earth. By loving God with all their heart, soul and mind and by loving one another, the presence-based community reveals the fullness of God's love and purposes on the earth. Rather than being defined by a doctrine or rules, the presence-based community is defined by love, truth, manifestation of the presence of God in signs and wonders, and care for those in need.

Instead of a weekly meeting, the new covenant Church is a presence-based community, a living fulfillment of the plan of God in which, as He said, "I will...walk among them. I will be their God, and they shall be My people" (2 Corinthians 6:16 NKJV).

Appendix A
12 Values of a Presence-Based Community

1. God is a Person.
  a.. The presence of God is personal; He has personality. (We were made in His image.)
  b. God loves you just as you are! (But, because of His love, He does not leave you that way!)
  c. The presence of God is transforming.
  c. The Bible is a Word of God (words) that reveals the Living Word of God (Spirit).

2. Worship is communication.
  a. We have an audience of One; in worship, our benefit is not the aim.
  b. Worship is corporate communion with God (adoration, thanksgiving and praise).
  c. God passionately seeks out those who worship (in spirit and truth).

3. Encounter is the reason for our gathering.
  a. Meeting with God is the primary reason that we gather (not for singing or the sermon, etc.).
  b. The first commandment is an activity that produces intimacy (loving God with *all* of us).
  c. The Bible is a book about encountering God. (Every story is about people encountering God.)
  d. When God shows up at the meeting, we won't have to worry about people coming.

4. Prayer is listening.
  a. Prayer is spiritual breathing. (It is essential for spiritual life.)
  b. Hearing God is essential to faith (faith comes by hearing).
  c. The Bible is a book about hearing God; people who hear God can respond properly.
  d. Talking to God before knowing what He wants is not prayer. We must know what to pray by listening before we respond.

5. Waiting on God is important.

a. Times of quietness are important times for interaction with God.

b. Being quiet is a way to "make room" for God to speak and move.

c. We are quiet (corporately) so that we can hear what He is saying (corporately).

d. We will not hear God if we pray by talking. We will hear only ourselves.

6. We are partners, not consumers.

a. Agreement with God produces partnership.

b. Partnership produces transformation.

c. When two or three agree with God, He will do it according to His will.

d. Partners are what God wants, not servants, friends or even sons.

e. Jesus is looking for a bride. A partner who loves to be with Him.

7. Hearing from God gives life.

a. God reveals Himself when He communicates.

b. Knowledge is not what we seek; we seek to know God.

c. From God we discover who we are and what we are here for.

8. Hearing from God creates responsibility.

a. Each member of the body of Christ must learn to hear God's voice.

b. The Word of God comes in such a way that we cannot ignore it.

c. The Word of God requires a response from us.

d. Obedience produces blessing; disobedience produces cursing.

e. All believers must practice good stewardship of the resources that God has given them.

9. Yieldedness is necessary for everything.

a. The only way to have a relationship with God is to yield your life to Him

b. The more yielded we are to God, the more He will use us

c. The only way to be great is to become servant of all

d. I am qualified to lead when I am content to serve

10. Fellowship is much more than eating together.

a. Fellowship is joined lives—we do *all* of life together, not just a meeting.

b. We live so that our lives are *non-optionally* joined together.

c. We will not pull back and disengage when we do not agree.

d. Listening and being present to one another IS our primary ministry to one another.

e. Fellowship is not based on agreement. It is based on love.

f. Forgiveness is necessary in all relationships.

11. Every member of the Body is essential.

a. God has given each member of the Body gifts and callings that are to be activated and must used to edify others.

b.Leaders serve others by leading them. They must be servants leaders.

c. God uses EACH member to love, encourage and sharpen the others.

12. Supernatural Ministry

a. God calls and empowers people to do things that they are unable to do without Him.

b. God has called and enabled each member of the church to make disciples like Jesus did.

c. Love is the basis for supernatural ministry not anointing.

d. God has called us to heal the sick and deliver the oppressed.

Endnotes

Chapter 1

1. James Strong, *Strong's Exhaustive Concordance of the Bible* (Nashville, Tennessee: Holman Bible Publishers, n.d.), #H6754.
2. Ibid., #H1823.
3. *Oxford Dictionary* Online, s.v. "personality," accessed March 2, 2021, https://en.oxforddictionaries.com/definition/personality.

Chapter 2

1. *Oxford Dictionary* Online, s.v. "free will," accessed March 2, 2021, https://en.oxforddictionaries.com/definition/free will.
2. Isaac Newton Quotes. BrainyQuote.com, BrainyMedia Inc, 2021. https://www.brainyquote.com/quotes/isaac_newton_753048, accessed March 12, 2021.

Chapter 3

1. *Online Etymology Dictionary*, s.v. "covenant," accessed March 2, 2021, https://www.etymonline.com/word/Covenant.

Chapter 4

1. Details about the Jewish Feast of Tabernacles in this paragraph are from "Yeshua and the Sukkot Water Drawing Festival" (June 1, 2016) One for Israel, https://www.oneforisrael.org/holidays/yeshua-and-the-sukkot-water-drawing-festival/.

Chapter 5

1. Stephen Gertz, "What is the pre-Christian history of the baptismal ceremony?" *Christianity Today*, August 8, 2008, https://www.christianitytoday.com/history/2008/august/what-is-pre-christian-history-of-baptismal-ceremony.html.
2. Cornelius J. Dyck, *Spiritual Life in Anabaptism: Classic Devotional Resources* (Scottsdale, Pennsylvania: Herald Press, 1995), 120.
3. C. Arnold Snyder, *Anabaptist History and Theology: Revised Student Edition* (Kitchener, Ontario: Pandora Press, 1977), 152.
4. James Strong, *Strong's Exhaustive Concordance of the Bible* (Nashville, Tennessee: Holman Bible Publishers, n.d.), #G4434.

Chapter 6

1. Barna Group, "Changes in Worldview Among Christians over the Past 13 Years," Research Releases in Faith and Christianity, March 9, 2009, https://www.barna.com/research/barna-survey-examines-changes-in-worldview-among-christians-over-the-past-13-years/.

2. Michael Brown, "The Strengths and Weaknesses of the American Church," *Charisma* Magazine, 2013, https://www.charismamag.com/life/culture/16419-the-strengths-and-weaknesses-of-the-american-church.

Chapter 7
1. J. H. Thayer, *Thayer's Greek Lexicon* (Public domain; Source: http://www.crosswire.org/sword/), #H2403.
2. Ibid., #H5771.
3. *Oxford Dictionary* Online, s.v. "worship," accessed March 6, 2021, https://en.oxforddictionaries.com/definition/worship.
4. Jacqueline Howard, "Americans devote more than 10 hours a day to screen time, and growing," CNN Health, July 29, 2016, https://www.cnn.com/2016/06/30/health/americans-screen-time-nielsen/index.html.

Chapter 8
1. James Strong, *Strong's Exhaustive Concordance of the Bible* (Nashville, Tennessee: Holman Bible Publishers, n.d.), #G1577.

Chapter 9
1. Theodore Roosevelt Quotes. BrainyQuote.com, BrainyMedia Inc, 2021. https://www.brainyquote.com/quotes/theodore_roosevelt_140484, accessed March 13, 2021.
2. *Ante-Nicene Fathers, Vol. 3, Latin Christianity: Its Founder, Tertullian* (Grand Rapids; Michigan: Wm B. Eerdmans Publishing Company, n.d.), Chapter 39, https://www.sacred-texts.com/chr/ecf/003/0030045.htm.
3. James Strong, *Strong's Exhaustive Concordance of the Bible* (Nashville, Tennessee: Holman Bible Publishers, n.d.), #H3519.
4. Ibid., #G4102.
5. Ibid., #G5486.

Chapter 10
1. James Strong, *Strong's Exhaustive Concordance of the Bible* (Nashville, Tennessee: Holman Bible Publishers, n.d.), #G4342.
2. Ibid., #G2842.
3. Ibid., #G3619.
4. All of the information in the preceding four paragraphs was taken from Justin Taylor, "What Was a Church Service Like in the Second Century?" The Gospel Coalition, August 29, 2010, https://www.thegospelcoalition.org/blogs/justin-taylor/what-was-a-church-service-like-in-the-second-century/. He paraphrased his information from N.R. Needham's *2,000 Years of Christ's Power, Vol. 1: Age of the Early Church Fathers.*
5. Strong, *Strong's Exhaustive Concordance of the Bible*, #G4245.
6. Ibid., #G1249.

CONTACT THE AUTHOR

If you're interested in having Jon speak at an event or conference in your community, please fill out the contact information using the link below.

Jon also provides coaching for church and ministry leaders to help them develop Presence-Based Community.

For more information or to fill out a coaching application, please visit: www.presencebasedcommunity.com/speaking